RAINCOAST CHRONICLES

LILIES & FIREWEED

FRONTIER WOMEN OF BRITISH COLUMBIA

STEPHEN HUME

PHOTO RESEARCH BY KATE BIRD

HARBOUR PUBLISHING

Published by
Harbour Publishing Co. Ltd.
P.O. Box 219, Madeira Park, BC
V0N 2H0
www.harbourpublishing.com
07 08 09 9 8 7 6 5 4 3
Text and cover design by Roger Handling
Cover illustration by Shelley Fearnley (inspired by a Mattie Gunterman photograph)
Title page image BC Archives B-00182

Printed and bound in Canada

Harbour Publishing acknowledges financial support from the Government of Canada through the Book Publishing Industry Development Program and the Canada Council for the Arts, and from the Province of British Columbia through the British Columbia Arts Council and the Book Publisher's Tax Credit through the Ministry of Provincial Revenue.

National Library of Canada Cataloguing in Publication

Hume, Stephen, 1947-
      Raincoast chronicles 20 : lilies and fireweed : frontier women of British Columbia / Stephen Hume.

Includes index.
Based on the series Frontier women, published in the Vancouver Sun, 2002.
ISBN 1-55017-313-8

      1. Women pioneers—British Columbia—Biography. 2. Frontier and pioneer life—British Columbia. 3. British Columbia—Biography. I. Title. II. Series: Frontier women

FC3805.H84 2004   971.1'0082   C2004-900913-3

Table of Contents

1 Pioneering through the Ages

Caril Chasens dwells in the same weather-beaten log cabin she built at McCully Creek with her own calloused hands about 30 winters ago at a place so far off the urban map that most of her fellow British Columbians couldn't find it if they tried. Living in a tent for shelter and later moving into a small lean-to that now sees duty as a recycling shed, she felled trees, bucked the logs with a chainsaw, then dragged them back to the building site with a long-departed Land Rover. Petite and still wiry as she approaches her sixties, her black hair now shot with silver, she winched the logs into place by hand using a come-along and then chinked the gaps between them with moss—although she later found that spun glass insulation tamped into the cracks does a far better job of keeping out the December wind.

Caril Chasens' pioneering spirit reaches back to B.C.'s origins. Leslie Barnwell

This tough frontier homesteader is a contemporary example of those courageous pioneer women whose often overlooked contributions shaped the cultural landscape, reformed our politics, defined who we are and made BC into a fully realized province. Like the lilies that settlers planted in their gardens, these women brought a domesticating, even exotic, aesthetic that spoke to the assumptions of a male-dominated society on a rough frontier. Yet the experiences of newcomers quickly meshed with the experiences of those who were

Chasens' 30-year-old log cabin, with more recent additions rising behind, is far from urban comforts.
Leslie Barnwell

**A gun, a dog and a pack horse—pio-
neer Mattie Gunterman leads her son
and husband into the bush.**
Mattie Gunterman Photo Vancouver Public
Library VPL 2213

indigenous and their collective influence
eventually proved as pervasive and as
hardy as the native fireweed that flour-
ishes everywhere—and most especially
in the aftermath of trial and hardship.

Today, Caril's original hexagonal
structure is graced with interesting add-
ons, one of them the studio where she
creates lustrous three-dimensional
metaphors from native woods. A naked
human form emerges from a carved
birch burl. A wood slab is transformed
into a bird perched on a log. A round
burl is sculpted into the flat realism of a
crab putting its claws up as it skitters
sideways through the ripples on a sandy
bottom. To reach this artist's modest

homestead in BC's remote outback, a vis-
itor by road must be prepared to travel
close to 1,200 kilometres north from
Vancouver, passing out of the electrified,
highly domesticated landscape of the

**Caril Chasens' tools transform slabs
of wood into luminous metaphors of
the wilderness life around her.**
Leslie Barnwell

Lower Mainland, through Prince
George, westward to Hazelton and
north, into a rugged world still illuminated mostly by starlight and sunshine.

This is a country where householders
encounter grizzlies in the garden, a place
where myths still have a tangible presence and the landscape itself thrums
with artistic intensity. Even the glittering
mountains have names and legends.
They thunder skyward out of the dark
shawl of the boreal forest with its lower
elevation embroideries of white birch
and crimson ground maple. Below them,
in villages like Kispiox, Kitseguecla,
Kitwanga and Kitwancool, is found the
richest concentration of totem pole art in
Canada. The jagged peaks of Hagwilget
and the more distant Seven Sisters are
high enough to make their own weather.
Their crags and icefields trail semi-per-
manent plumes of cloud and the icy

meltwater from their glaciers primes the vast hydraulics of a dark green Skeena River and its cold, swift, salmon-bearing tributaries. But for now, the focus comes down to this logging road, our muddy four-by-four still bouncing and juddering northward over ruts and potholes as the gravel surrenders to dirt and the bridges dwindle to a narrow single-lane span. Telephone poles and cables vanished some time back. Now the bush closes in. Another 50 kilometres of this, up over the ridge and we'd be into the upper Nass watershed.

I'm here looking for the woman I hope will provide one of those elusive, living connections between ourselves and the frontier experienced by pioneer women 150 years ago. "Frontier" is a loaded word, of course. It comes charged with the energy of countless justifying icons from North America's paternalistic and colonial past. Traditionally, the frontier is the edge along which "wilderness" defines "civilization." It is also the place where the colonizing culture that presumes itself predestined for dominance most often encounters the unwelcome reality of that dispersed rural "other" that continues to pose vigorous alternatives to urban comfort and refinement. When I set out to try and shape some kind of narrative from the diverse experiences of women whose lives on the geographical frontier had helped bring into being the modern province we call British Columbia, I soon discovered that these women also dwelt on a metaphysical frontier.

Their lives were lived at the boundaries of what would come to shape our notions of a just, pluralistic and egalitarian society, of economic culture and political philosophy as well. And all had one clear thing in common: except for a few exotic celebrities, they were virtually absent from the historic records assembled, for the most part, by their male contemporaries.

The records of missionaries, fur traders, literary men, and the keepers of church and government documents, the writings of brothers, sons, fathers, and husbands are the main sources of women's history, point out Beth Light and Alison Prentice in their 1980 collection, *The Pioneer Women of British North America, 1713–1867*. "Unfortunately, where the women themselves have been totally silent, such records are some-times our only sources and we must read between the lines for the reality of women's historical lives," they note.

I soon discovered that the story of BC's frontier women was fragmented, scattered and sometimes difficult to find, even "between the lines." Some of it I

Mattie Gunterman ventured into BC mining camps, working as a cook, trapper and subsistence farmer, while documenting life in a collection of glass-plate negatives. The pre-World War I images recorded by Gunterman—seen here near Beaton about 1900—came into wider circulation thanks to Henri Robideau's *Flapjacks and Photographs: A History of Mattie Gunterman, Camp Cook and Photographer.*
Mattie Gunterman Photo Vancouver Public Library VPL 2215

Poet Pauline Johnson dressed as a Mohawk Princess, a nickname many people used for her.
BC Archives A-09684

found in dusty, long unopened record boxes in city and provincial archives, some in museum exhibits, some in microfilmed obituaries and wedding notices, some by dogging used bookstores for long-out-of-print local histories. Until recently, women's own voices often emerged from the history of the day only as footnotes, brief asides, amused anecdotes, secondary references or quotations from forgotten journals, letters, memoirs, household accounts and family stories. Yet, as I stitched my quilt together from these brightly coloured bits and pieces, the narrative began to take on a fascinating and astonishing texture of its own.

"The History of a Country is written from the lives of Men, but from the lives of the Women we learn best of a Nation's soul," observes one rare, detailed, early account of women's stories dating back to 1843 that was found for me, perhaps appropriately, in a quaint glass cabinet at the back of his store by Adrian Batterbury, proprietor of the quirky antiquarian establishment in Sidney named The Haunted Book Shop. Published in 1928 by the Women's Canadian Club of Victoria and out of print ever since (a planned second volume apparently foundered with the stock market crash of 1929 and the onset of the Great Depression), *The Pioneer Women of Vancouver Island, 1843–1866* was written "In order that we, and those who follow us, may remember the courage, strength of purpose and nobility of character which governed the lives of the pioneer women of Vancouver Island." *Women of British Columbia*, the next comprehensive look at their collective history, was undertaken almost half a century later by Jan Gould, the popular Vancouver Island historian. Indeed, before the 1970s—just about the time Caril Chasens was building her cabin—there was little serious study of women's history as a formal discipline. Between the publication of that first volume and

Gould's book, the history of frontier women in our province had largely moved out of living memory and into the archival record.

In recent years, however, the rise of an assertive feminist scholarship has brought new perspectives and a new appreciation of women's history to the fore. Today few universities have no women's history component in the curriculum and, in the tradition of BC's own Margaret Ormsby, some of our best historians are now women—Jean Barman, Patricia Roy, Lynne Bowen and the generation that will succeed them. And yet in the bigger sweep of things, the study of women's history remains a relatively fresh phenomenon. On my writing table, the books from which I've gleaned much of the background about BC's remarkable frontier women now number well over 100. Many mention no women in their indexes, even when the books contain references in their narratives—the assumption being, I guess, that nobody would want to look them up. But some offer dramatic first-person accounts of great adventures, of incredible hardships, of courage, of bravery, of tenderness and indomitable will in the face of tragedies and tribulations that would have broken many.

A Nakoaktok chief's daughter.
BC Archives D-08311

Front, from left: Agnes McKay, Lilias Spalding. Rear: Charles Lowe, Gerry Payne, Arthur Spalding, Arthur Lowe on Pender Island, 1889
BC Archives B-07186

The frontier for women left a complicated legacy of many changeable faces. For First Nations women, it wasn't a frontier at all. It was a contemporary modernity that was about to change forever. To find Native pioneers, you'd have to look back to 6,000, or perhaps even 10,000 or 20,000, years ago. For women from Europe and Asia who came so long afterward, initially crossing the oceans in vermin-infested sailing vessels that had to battle their way around Cape Horn, or beating eastward against the tireless North Pacific trade winds, the frontier ranged from the elegant boudoirs of a new colonial capital to the brothel cribs of brutal mining camps.

The frontier was multicultural long before we invented the word, an amazing mosaic of more than 35 aboriginal nations and languages, of Iroquois, Cree and Ojibway women who came with the fur trade, Scots who travelled the lonely back country like fur-clad ghosts, Métis paddlers, Hawaiians, Chinese miners and Japanese mill hands, Portuguese and Italians, English officers, American merchants, Finnish fishermen and Swedish loggers, German dance hall girls, Blacks turning their backs on a slave state, Sikhs and Hindus, Muslims and Jews, Roman Catholics, Anglicans and Methodists. The frontier for women was found equally in classrooms and medical wards, on the factory floor and at the pithead, in painting, poetry, politics and

Graduating class of nurses at Vancouver General Hospital in 1909.
City of Vancouver Archives CVA 677-507

An antique by uptown standards, the wood-fired cookstove is a reliable essential in the backcountry.
Leslie Barnwell

sports. While much is made today of women's hockey, who remembers that the game in BC was pioneered by a feisty women's team that travelled from Victoria to Dawson City to play in 1904?

Then there were the questions of where the frontier era ends and whom among the hundreds of candidates to include in the narrative. I decided, somewhat arbitrarily, that World War I marked the great transformation of BC from its rural, agrarian roots to the industrialized urban giant it is today. So I made 1914 the cutoff point. As for whom to mention, that too was necessarily arbitrary because of the volume of material. Generally, I opted for those less well known, except for women whose ground-breaking work insisted upon their inclusion. And to further complicate things, it turns out that the frontier isn't an artifact that's been fossilized in an unchanging past. It's with us yet, in both geographical and metaphysical terms.

Caril Chasens is an example of this. I found her deep in the forest, far from the entertainments and diversions most of us take for granted, where she lives cheerfully under conditions that most of her big-city sisters couldn't abide. She hauls water for washing and cooking from the tumbling creek beyond her back door, tramping the summer trail with a pair of plastic buckets until freeze-up. Then she switches to the winter trail, which leads to a more distant point where the current in McCully Creek is swift enough to preclude ice formation. Even the most rugged individuals generally balk at chopping their water at 30 below zero. What Caril and her partner Geoff Watling do have to chop are the many cords of firewood and bales of kindling necessary for cooking and heating their cabin during the long, dark, often bitter months they must spend waiting out winter deep in the northern Interior. At the time I met with Caril, winter had been holding off. "In the old days, you had snow by the first of November," she says. "Winters were fiercer then. But this winter's just not happening. It makes it gloomy around here when all the leaves are gone and there's no snow on the ground. Maybe it's global warming. Maybe not. It's amazing how different the climate is from spot to spot."

Caril lives well beyond the ubiquitous electricity grid that most of us assume is essential for normal life. To communicate with the outside she uses a radio telephone. The only street lights are the shimmering green and yellow curtains of the aurora borealis. The only electrical energy comes from a small gasoline generator supplemented by some solar panels and it's husbanded for power tools and the computer. There's no dishwasher, no electric range, no baseboard heaters, no PlayStation 2 to while away a dreary evening. "One plus is that you don't give a damn when the power goes out or the phone service quits," says Caril, dark eyes flashing, shrugging a little deeper into her red plaid shirt. "The worst thing is trying to fix your truck and breaking a part and having to drive an hour of gravel to get another one." Behind her, the kitchen counter is fragrant with new loaves. She bakes her own bread every week, one more way of avoiding the fuel costs of that long drive to the nearest convenience store. That's in Kispiox, a Gitksan

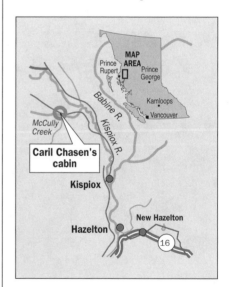

village of 651 or 553, depending upon whom you ask. "These roads just beat vehicles to death," she says. Indeed, the hulks of several that have already died are out at the fringes of the yard. Willows sucker up through the windows.

And yet, despite similarities that her pioneer sisters from two centuries ago would recognize instantly, any woman who chooses the frontier life in BC in the 21st century has a far different experience from one who lived in the early years of this province. "I'm as much in the 21st century as any woman in Manhattan—a little less worried about bombers, perhaps. I'm marketing my art on the Internet. It connects me directly into the mainstream," Caril says. Her partner, on the other hand, a 20-year veteran of the forest industry who says he reinvented himself as a computer nerd when the bottom fell out of logging, uses the household computer to operate a digital recording studio for musicians scattered up the Kispiox Valley.

"We're not separate from the world here. There was a time when I believed you could get back to nature, get back to that hippy-dippy paradise we thought was over the horizon," she says. "Now, I know, problems are global. I used to think I could get away from them, but you can't. You are part of it wherever you go." In fact, she points out, this very afternoon there's an air quality warning out from Environment Canada for the whole zone between Terrace and Smithers, an area the size of some small European countries. People are warned to avoid strenuous activity outdoors because of the particulate matter in the air from mills and slash burning. "Yes, it's a different way of living out here on McCully Creek but it's definitely not the 1800s," she observes, waving a hand dismissively. "Actually, I'm thankful for that. I wouldn't want to go back there, anyway. It was real crappy for women back then." Born in Dayton, Ohio, in 1945, she came to Canada in 1966 and drifted north until she wound up here, in a curve of this little singing tributary of the Kispiox, surrounded by the forests, mountains and sky that inspire and infuse her art.

Like Caril, many of those earlier pioneer women came to BC in search of greater freedom, with dreams of a new life beyond the reach of stifling conventions, a chance for greater prosperity, for the opportunity to fulfill themselves creatively and make a better future for their own children than they had faced in Europe, Asia and America. Like her, they encountered unimaginably hard work and difficult conditions, which they accepted, then mastered, then turned to their own advantage. Yet a woman on the frontier today is still within a helicopter flight of first-class medical treatment, even if it means slamming over frozen ruts in a four-by-four to get to a landing site. A century ago, many rural inhabi-

tants might have had to travel a week to find a doctor. For women of childbearing years, this added risks to their lives that most young women today would consider unacceptable. For every 1,000 births, five women and 120 babies would die. In 1871, the average woman could expect to have 6.8 children and the majority of those women lived on rural farmsteads, in logging shows, fishing outports and mining camps—far beyond the reach of medical care and technology that we today assume as a birthright. What they endured is a reminder of the significance of their contributions to the creation of this province.

As for Caril? How far is she from town?

"How far? I don't know," she says, bemused by the question. "I've never measured."

And that, perhaps, is the true measure of a frontier woman—one who's gone so far beyond the comforts and predictabilities of urban life that she can't remember the distance back.

Camp life meant hard work and difficult conditions for women.
Mattie Gunterman Photo Vancouver Public Library VPL 2214

2 Mothers of the Old World

In its official form, the documentary history of women in British Columbia can be said to begin at Tatoosh Island, where a honey-shouldered wedge of cretaceous sediment tilts out of the storm-tossed entrance to the Strait of Juan de Fuca. Bearing the name of an aboriginal chief, this island is the most westerly location in Washington State and therefore a point of pilgrimage for Americans who northwest up the Olympic Peninsula to the territory of the Makah—famous in the past as great whalers, infamous to some in the present for their impertinent renewal of that whaling tradition.

The tourists stop to pick up their $11 recreation permits in the Makah community at Neah Bay, where the pavement finally gives way to potholes and gravel, continue past the fish nets drying in the wind outside an old military base recycled for tribal administration purposes, then park their cars and hike the rest of the way to Cape Flattery along a trail maintained by the band. The footpath winds through waist-deep salal, nodding ferns and a sighing rain forest

Nootka women on the beach with clam baskets on their backs, awaiting the tide to fall and uncover the clam beds.
BC Archives D-08313

A Clayoquot girl smiles from under a blanket (left), while another (right) gazes from beneath cedar branches. It was the custom for girls to wear a mask of boughs for one year upon reaching womanhood.
Glenbow Archives NA-1700-79 and NA-181-69

that was already old when the images of the wives of Chief Tatoosh were graven by a Spanish explorer over 210 years ago. Today, chainsawed tree rounds make stepping stones through soft spots and boardwalks, constructed from planks as thick as Danielle Steel paperbacks, lift walkers over fragile ground and past cedars still bearing marks where bark was stripped to make clothing and baskets for rituals and ceremonies.

Eventually, hikers emerge at a spectacular clifftop lookout. To the north, the ragged graveyard coast of Vancouver Island continues westward, the shore fringed with white lace, the mountains scabbed with vast clear-cuts and draped in cloud. Below, translucent green swells off the Swiftsure Bank boom into sea caves and cause the whole promontory to shudder underfoot.

Most visitors come to take in the scenery and look for the bright orange bills of the exotic tufted puffins that nest on the cliffs, maybe even spot a big shark or sea mammal drawn by the abundant marine life that congregates to feed on nutrients welling up from the underwater canyons just offshore. Few of the visitors that I asked knew that it was from this precise lookout that the Makah first saw the ships carrying European mariners who would give us our earliest documentary glimpse of the society of women who occupied the unknown landscape west of the Rockies.

Traders and explorers from the French and American colonies had penetrated deep into the interior of the continent by the mid-18th century, but BC was unknown, unmapped and as remote from Europe as the dark side of the moon. Yet before the first adventurers arrived, this area of the continent was a quilt of nations, their territories defined by geography, by linguistic affiliation, by

Women of Ahousat on Flores Island in Clayoquot Sound gather on a bench with the next generation.
BC Archives H-07195

trading hegemonies, by transportation routes, by political alliances and by war. Women, as they still were for European royalty and had been for Bronze Age warlords, Chinese and Roman emperors, Egyptian Pharaohs, Persian satraps, African rulers and Aztec god-kings, were a crucial factor in forging dynastic alliances by marriage. In short, women of rank were a political commodity as well as a vital and sustaining part of the community. They were also prized booty, frequently taken and held as slaves in war. In fairness, there are some early Russian references from the North Coast, a fleeting description of Haida women and their dress in the journals of Juan Josef Perez Hernandez who sailed from California to the Queen Charlotte Islands in 1774 and a brief account of Nuu-chah-nulth culture by James Cook four years later at Friendly Cove. For the most part, despite their importance aboriginal women are even less of a presence in the documentary record than their

European sisters. Even today, after a full generation of feminism and raging gender politics in the academy, entries for women are to be found in few indexes of current anthropological and sociological studies of aboriginal cultures.

In the sketches of Manuel José Antonio Cardero, however, an artist attached to a Spanish expedition that stopped at Neah Bay in 1792, some of that missing history springs to vivid life in the faces of the wives of Tatoosh. He had three that we know about—evidence of his wealth and stature—and we know that his relationship with them was infused with affection. When he was invited aboard a Spanish ship and offered a cup of cocoa, Tatoosh drank some and then insisted on taking the rest to one of his wives waiting in the canoe alongside—the crew called her Maria— so that she could share in the novel taste.

Back then, of course, there was no BC, no Washington State, no Canada, even the United States of America was a

precarious experiment involving 13 tiny colonies on the far side of the continent. But there were the Makah, the southern cousins of the powerful Nuu-chah-nulth nation whose political, linguistic and cultural hegemony extended down the entire western shore of Vancouver Island. So it seems appropriate that any narrative about pioneer women, their lives and their accomplishments should begin at Tatoosh Island because, like the astonishing array of nations and cultures that existed here before the influx of Europeans, Asians, Africans and South Sea Islanders, the society of women sprawls across the artificially imposed boundaries of politics, ethnicity, geography and history.

The notion of "pioneer" women in BC is an oxymoron that begins with an assumption that history here is short and commences with the arrival of those whose cultures subsequently came to dominate the social and political landscape. But history here is ancient.

Maria and her husband Chief Tatoosh as sketched by Manuel José Antonio Cardero in 1792.
University of Washington Special Collections U23484Z and NA23483Z

Radiocarbon datings from the earliest excavated sites of human habitation in BC average more than 10,500 years before present. Some from a large animal kill in Washington push the date back another 2,000 years. To put that into historical perspective, women had already been looking after their families and maintaining their households in BC for at least 7,000 years by the time Moses led his people out of Egypt.

For me, the idea of the earliest pioneer women in BC evokes two images. The first is from a remarkable series of films about the Netsilikmiut of the Central Arctic made half a century ago by the brilliant National Film Board producer and cinematographer Doug Wilkinson. In a segment entitled "Going to the Weir," the camera focusses on a vast panorama of brown tundra beneath a cold sky. Only after many minutes does the observer become aware that there is indeed something happening. Those specks on the horizon looming larger and then dwindling again in the distance are a family walking toward the camera on their way to a favoured fishing spot. This is how it must have been for the first pioneer women trekking across the land bridge of Beringia, burdened with

A Cowichan woman tying a bundle of reeds, 1912.
Glenbow Archives NA-1700-49

equipment and supplies, keeping track of children, entertaining them, setting up and breaking down camp while the male hunters ranged ahead in the immense, hostile landscape in search of the next meal, sometimes not returning for days and expecting to be fed and serviced when they did. Work may differ in a wage economy, but divisions of labour respecting the family today are not so different from then, if the sociological surveys can be believed. Women still run most households, particularly with respect to food acquisition and preparation, and manage the nurturing and education of children.

On the other hand, a growing number of scholarly adherents supports the theory that the first pioneers to the West Coast came not by land but by sea. Some North Coast stories among aboriginal peoples make references to a specific number of people crossing from Siberia to Alaska in a skin boat in flight from some dimly remembered tribal conflict—which brings to mind the second image, shared by an RCMP officer on the Arctic Coast. He told of watching a skin kayak with a lone paddler making its way to shore. At the beach, he said, the paddler disembarked, followed by his children, then five dogs and finally his wife—a reminder that the first woman to pioneer here may well have arrived the same way.

But how did these women live? Indications can be gleaned from the artifacts on display at the Makah Cultural and Research Center in Neah Bay. This stunning assemblage of 30,000 pieces was excavated at the Ozette River, where six houses from a village of 800 Makah

Preparing meals was a daily task for both women and children.
Glenbow Archives NA-1141-19

A Nakoaktok woman gathers abalones in the Seymour Inlet area. Glenbow Archives NA-1700-63

were buried in a mudslide 500 years before Christopher Columbus and then exposed again in 1970. The clay tomb sealed out oxygen and preserved perishables that would otherwise have long ago rotted away. It also created an intimate archeological snapshot of life in each house at the moment of burial—a record made of tools and implements, clothing, furniture, housewares, foodstuffs, ornaments and weapons. They suggest a strenuous life dictated by the coming and going of fish, birds and sea mammals. If the men were whalers and warriors, the women were custodians of family life. In stratified coastal societies that ranked people as nobility, commoners and slaves—a hierarchy not so different from those of the European newcomers—it's probably safe to conclude that aboriginal women had influence, but not power. And that influence would be graduated according to the rank and power of one's family and husband.

One North Coast woman, the daughter of a chief, took the name "Chief of All Women" when she was married by arrangement to another powerful chief to cement a dynastic alliance. Another, whose name is lost to history, was herself chief of the Nahannis when she intervened to save Fort Liard factor Robert Campbell from starvation in 1837. "She was a fine looking woman above the middle height and about 35 years old," Campbell reported to the Hudson's Bay Company. "She had a pleasing face lit up with intelligent eyes, which when she was excited flashed with fire. She was tidy and tasteful in her dress. At our first meeting she was accompanied by some of her tribe and her husband, who was a non-entity." The Nahanni chief must have been a powerful and respected leader because she openly defied Chief Shakes, who controlled the flow of furs from the Stikine watershed and was forcing trade to the Russians, for whom he served as the regional middleman. It's interesting to note that Campbell's observations focus on her beauty rather than her political power. Perez, too, commented on the beauty of Haida women he observed but also noted that "they gave signs of meekness and good

Upper Kootenay woman and baby in a cradle board in Windermere. Glenbow Archives NA-1135-18

Nakoaktok woman paints a hat of a form borrowed from the Haida. The Nakoaktok were a Kwakiutl tribe residing at Seymour Inlet. Glenbow Archives NA-1700-64

At Birth

I used to help at times of birth, yes,
I used to help all the women around here.
I learned it from my book, my blue doctor's book.
I used to read it all the time.

I made up my mind that if she needs help,
I will help her. I'm not scared.
You've got to be awfully quick. There's two lives there.
The baby and the mother.

Yes, two lives, and what you got to do it with
Those days? You've got to be quick
To cut the cord, keep the bed clean, take out
The afterbirth, discard it, burn it.

Yes, you've got to be quick, fix the baby,
Tie its navel so it will not bleed

Photograph taken in 1973 of Mary Augusta Tappage, author of *The Days of Augusta*.
Robert Keziere

To death—cut it about that long.
When it heals there's nothing left, you know.

Then you bandage the mother, pin her up,
Keep her clean, keep her in bed ten days.
The doctor told us this—but if I leave
I guess she got up.

I never had to spank a baby
To make him cry—they always cried.
They were always alive and healthy.
Yes, mother and baby, alive and healthy.

by Mary Augusta Tappage 1888–1978
From *The Days of Augusta*, edited by Jean E. Speare

disposition," qualities doubtless desirable to the male-dominated cultures of Europe. A Spanish botanist and naturalist named José Mariano Mozino kept notes when he was dispatched to do scientific work for Juan Francisco de la Bodega y Quadra, who had been sent to explore the "limits to the north of California" in 1792. He described in detail the dress and ornamentation of Nuu-chah-nulth women.

But it's the Makah museum—with its assemblage of baskets, each designed for a special purpose, its specialized utensils for food preparation and presentation, its examples of cedar bark clothing, a dog-hair blanket adorned with woodpecker feathers and woven in a plaid pattern reminiscent of old Highland tartans, and even the loom on which such fabric was woven—that tells the most exact and engaging story of women's lives. It's clear that women had a central role in the collection of raw materials for the manufacture of these utensils and in gathering, preparing and putting up foodstuffs for the winter. There were

clams to be smoked, berries to be picked, seagull eggs to be gathered, fish to be cleaned, dried and smoked, the mysterious little "Ozette potatoe" to be dug, cedar bark to be stripped and processed, blankets to be woven.

According to Makah custom, much of the food preparation and the protocols of hospitality were supervised by the senior female member of the family. This was complicated, since each dish was governed by rules regarding preparation, presentation, service and appropriate ceremony. She and her subordinates were responsible for ensuring that visitors were served according to the strict privileges of their rank, that small children were fed next and finally that none of the remaining guests left hungry. This responsibility was a daunting one, considering that Nuu-chah-nulth chief Maquinna, for example, expected 36 different dishes to be served to guests at his formal banquets. One of those events sat Captains Quadra and George Vancouver at the same table and helped defuse the tensions that had brought the empires of

Baskets woven by West Coast Native women were beautifully designed but also practical for daily use.
Glenbow Archives NA-1807-8

Spain and Britain to the brink of war over their colonial claims to the West Coast. The name of the Nuu-chah-nulth woman who managed that banquet of international diplomacy that helped lay the foundations for what's now BC is lost to formal history, but like the wives of Tatoosh who greeted the Spanish in what's now Washington, she can certainly be said to have helped pioneer the birth of a new world.

3 The Accidental Tourist

Scattered across Barkley Sound like jade and silver beads from a shattered necklace, the Broken Group archipelago provides a stunningly beautiful maze of sheltered passages and white shell beaches in waters that teem with marine life. And it was near here, at Bamfield, just before mid-summer almost 220 years ago, with the light of the northern latitudes lying long on the swells rolling in from China, that the sailing ship *Imperial Eagle* dropped anchor and the first non-aboriginal woman of whom we're certain—Frances Hornby Barkley—arrived in what would become British Columbia.

First Nations households like the one sketched by John Webber at Nootka Sound were large and demanded complex management skills of the women who ran them.
BC Archives PDP 00235

There is a legendary tale from Clo-oose that in the mid-1700s a Spanish ship visited the west coast of Vancouver Island. It might possibly have been an early voyage of exploration—some believe both Sir Francis Drake and a Spanish expedition piloted by Juan de Fuca visited these shores more than 400 years ago. More likely, however, any such vessel would have been a galleon sailing between South America and the Philippines that had been blown off course by a storm and found itself with BC's graveyard coast as a fatal lee shore. In any event, the legend goes that the crew was killed and a group of Spanish women were made captives by the Nitinat people, became integrated into tribal life and later bore children. But many decades afterward when another Spanish vessel passed, the captives stole a canoe and fled. There's no mention of this in any known Spanish maritime records, so the story is likely apocryphal or the anachronistic appropriation of some other incident. On the other hand, it's reported that some Ditidaht and Nitinat people have found glass, bits of jewellery, fragments of gold chain and even a Spanish lady's comb in the San Juan River.

the glare of a tropical sun on the sea in which Element, they pass so much of their time the Women have no pretentions to beauty. but they are very active and lively, and also healthy, I did not see any vestiges amongst them of Leprosy, which we remarked amongst the Men of Owhyhee. we were surprised to find so few articles of curiosity amongst them but the Feathered Cloaks & Helmets are only worn by the Chiefs and the King. who appears to Rule the whole of the Groups of Islands Called by Capt Cook Sandwich Islands the Kings name when we Visited Oahy hee — was Tomahomehaw a perfect savage —

The last page of Frances Barkley's "Reminiscences." [from *The Remarkable World of Frances Barkley: 1769–1845*] BC Archives

Captain Charles Barkley took a teenaged bride on his trading voyage into the unknown.
Vancouver Public Library VPL 39031

For the more formal purposes of history, however, the first female European for whom documentary proof exists arrived on the west coast of Vancouver Island in late June, 1787. Frances Barkley was 17 and newly wed to Charles W. Barkley, the master of a 20-gun square-rigger of 400 tonnes sailing under Austrian colours to evade British trading licences. In the previous 18 months, Barkley had sailed halfway around the world to barter for the sea otter pelts he planned to sell in China before backhauling exotic Oriental cargoes to Europe. On the voyage, Barkley accidentally discovered the "lost" Strait of Juan de Fuca—Nuu-chah-nulth, Nitinat, Ditidaht and Makah mariners laugh at the notion it was ever either lost or discovered in the first place—and left his own name on the enormous sound that lies between Ucluelet and Bamfield.

Fanny, as she was called by her husband, must have been a feisty teenaged bride.

While there was a robust history of

Opposite: Frances Barkley cast off a life of luxury when she moved into the cramped quarters of the *Imperial Eagle* and set off on a journey around the world.
Illustration by Captain Steve Mayo

British women going to sea—from the notorious pirates Anne Bonny and Mary Read to women serving as cooks on whaling ships and trading vessels, at least a dozen female sailors are known from the 18th and early 19th centuries—a mariner's life was brutal, dangerous and frequently abbreviated by the privations of wretched food, bad water, storms and attacks by Natives. The *Imperial Eagle*, for instance, lost six men to a Makah ambush at the mouth of the Hoh River in 1787 and the following year John Meares was approached by a strange canoe in Friendly Cove and offered the mummified hand of what he thought must be the remains of one of the victims since one of the paddlers was wearing an item that had belonged to Barkley's second mate.

It was, however, far from common for a proper young English lady to accompany her husband to sea in the face of such possibilities. Indeed, British admiralty regulations issued in 1731 and again in 1756 expressly forbade women from going to sea aboard Royal Navy ships without specific orders from the most senior officers. Fanny was only 16 and a clergyman's daughter fresh out of convent school when she met Charles William Barkley, then aged 25. Five weeks later, on October 27, 1786, she

married him in the chapel at Ostend and, defying tradition, insisted on joining him on his voyage, since naval regulations had no bearing on a merchant ship under a foreign flag. And so, about 1 p.m. on November 24, she waved farewell to her father as the *Imperial Eagle* slipped its moorings and caught the ebb tide.

It would not be a pleasure cruise. Even the best ships of the day were foul, leaky, rat-infested tubs, the bilges reeking of filth, the sleeping quarters often soaked and the rations dreadful. Although scurvy was in retreat by the time Fanny Barkley followed her husband to sea, sailors were routinely afflicted by various fevers, respiratory infections, dysentery and smallpox. A Royal Navy casualty report of the day shows that between 1776 and 1798, less than 2,000 men died in the 10 battles fought by its fleets during the Revolutionary and Napoleonic wars while 85,000 died of disease, shipboard accidents and shipwrecks.

Living in a tiny cabin with all her domestic possessions in a single locker beneath her hard, narrow bunk, sharing the cramped saloon with the first mate as well as the captain, she circumnavigated the world twice with her husband, bore and buried children at sea and kept a

"Our dear little Patty died on board. . ."

My beloved Husband was attacked with a dreadful disease, which is common to these Climats, a violent Colic but with the most extraordinary symptoms, and excruciating pain, attended with fever and distortions of every kind. Two Men could hardly restrain him, so as to prevent his hurting himself. He turned all colours, sometimes appearing as if Actually dead. After a time the symptoms abated, and he got over it, but it left him in a dreadfully debilitated state. But a similar disease deprived us of our dear little Patty, then a twelve Month old, saving one day. She died on board the Halcyon on the 15th day of April, 1791 or 92. A Leaden Box was prepared for her remains in order that they might be kept until we could Inter her remains in consicrated ground, in some Dutch settlement, and accordingly we made for the Island of Celebes. When after much negociation with the unfeeling Dutch Resident, and extortions of every kind, She was laid in a burying Ground situated opposite the place where we were at Anchor, from whence we watched the Ceremony, not being allowed to go on shore to pay the last duties to our dear Child. The spot where she is deposited is one of the most beautiful in the World—as are all the Spice Islands. There she lies under the Shade of a Grove of Cocoa Nut Trees.

—from Frances Hornby Barkley's *Reminiscences* (as quoted in the Beth Hill text), written at the age of 66 and based on the diary of her circumnavigations of the globe

Vancouver Island's remote west coast soon became the hub of a vigorous trans-Pacific trading network.
BC Archives A-02688

vivid and lively diary of her experiences. The surviving correspondence between Fanny and Charles reveals a deep and abiding affection over 46 years of marriage. Although Frances Island, Mount Hornby and Trevor Channel, the main entrance to Port Alberni, were all named in her honour by her husband, Fanny Barkley fell into obscurity. Like the enigmatic legend of the Spanish women at Clo-oose, however, Fanny Barkley's story has its own mystery.

When the late Beth Hill, a Victoria writer known for her studies of Indian petroglyphs, was researching a rock carving of a sailing ship found at Clo-oose, she noted that Captain Walbran said he had consulted Frances Barkley's diary in the preparation of his great scholarly work from 1909, *British Columbia Coast Names, 1592–1906*. He'd borrowed the diary from her grandson, Captain Edward Barkley, who had settled at Westholme, near Crofton on the east side of Vancouver Island. Then Hill found a story in the *Victoria Daily*

Colonist newspaper reporting that shortly after Walbran returned the diary in 1909, Barkley's house had caught fire. Barkley was killed when he rushed back into the burning building in an attempt to retrieve some papers of great importance. The Barkley diary vanished and was presumed destroyed in the blaze.

But when Hill travelled to England to interview descendants while researching her book *The Remarkable World of Frances Barkley: 1769–1845*, she found correspondence that makes a compelling

case that this diary survived until at least 1952. Today it's possibly sitting on the bookshelf of someone who doesn't know its importance. The literary trail petered out when Hill died in 1997, leaving unsolved the conundrum of Fanny Barkley's lost diary, a mystery as fascinating as the story of the castaway Spanish women of Clo-oose.

"They came singing their War Song. . ."

Once, in particular, Captn B. saw several War Canoes with his Night Glass, stealing along under the shadow of the land on a fine moonlight Night, and as we were very indifferently Man'd, he was suspicious of their intention, and therefore he had a whole Broad side fired off over their heads, which made a great noise amongst the trees. We heard them scuttle off, but kept perfect silence on board that they might not think we were alarmed. Early the next morning they came alongside dreassed in their War dresses, and singing their War Song & keeping time with their paddles. When they had paddled three times round the vessel they set up a great Shout, then pulled off their masks and resumed their usual habits, and exhibited their sea otter skins, and gave us to understand they had been on a war expedition and had taken them from their Enemies. They never alluded to the firing, but went on trading as if nothing had passed, firing off their own Muskets in the Air, and then giving a great Shout.

—from Frances Hornby Barkley's *Reminiscences*, on an incident at Nootka Sound in 1792

4 The First, First Lady

Over 175 years ago, just beyond the palisades of the fur trading outpost Fort St. James, established by Simon Fraser in 1806, the courage of a shy young woman who kept a cool head during a terrifying crisis was to change the course of history. Situated on the southeast end of Stuart Lake, about 950 kilometres by road north of Vancouver, this small community of 2,046 people is an important Carrier First Nations settlement. But Fort St. James also ranks as the second-oldest continuously inhabited European settlement in the province. For nearly 40 years before Victoria was founded far to the south, Fort St. James would serve as the capital of New Caledonia, the British colony that comprised much of the Interior. Indeed, the British Columbia we know today might not have come to pass without the intervention of that young woman.

Amelia was the daughter of William Connolly, the Hudson's Bay Company's chief factor at Fort St. James, and Miyo Nipiy, a Cree woman. In 1828 she married a junior fur trader serving at the fort named James Douglas. Douglas had destiny printed in his soul. He would later found Fort Victoria, help blunt the American expansionism that would wrest much of the Oregon Territory from the Crown, secure British interests on the Pacific Slope, manage the turbulent gold rush of 1858, sign treaties with First Nations in a far-sighted policy later abandoned by greedy politicians, serve as midwife for the union of New

Fort St. James village, shown in the 1890s, had been a fur trading post since 1806 and was the capital of New Caledonia for almost 40 years.
BC Archives A-04241

Caledonia with Vancouver Island and end his career as the governor who presided over the birth of responsible, democratic government. But in 1828, Douglas was merely a brash and ambitious young clerk whose intelligence and skill had already come to the attention of his superiors but whose worth had yet to be proven.

The story of James and Amelia Douglas points to a fascinating moment that winked into existence about 200 years ago on the west side of the Rocky Mountains and then flickered out in the ruins of a human catastrophe of epic proportions. For a moment, it seemed that the collision of European and aboriginal cultures was about to bring forth

Portrait of Lady Amelia Douglas, circa 1865.
BC Archives A-02834

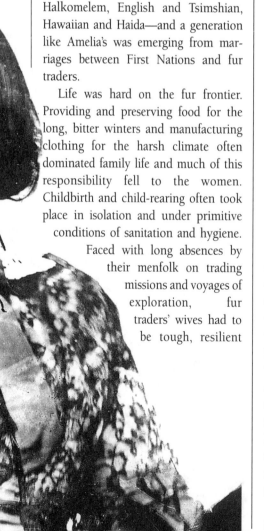

Indian women packers at Moricetown, near Smithers, in the early 1900s.
BC Archives A-06062

something entirely new. A common language was being born—Chinook, the language of commerce forged from French and Mowachaht, Spanish and Halkomelem, English and Tsimshian, Hawaiian and Haida—and a generation like Amelia's was emerging from marriages between First Nations and fur traders.

Life was hard on the fur frontier. Providing and preserving food for the long, bitter winters and manufacturing clothing for the harsh climate often dominated family life and much of this responsibility fell to the women. Childbirth and child-rearing often took place in isolation and under primitive conditions of sanitation and hygiene.

Faced with long absences by their menfolk on trading missions and voyages of exploration, fur traders' wives had to be tough, resilient and resourceful in an often hostile environment.

Aboriginal women who had been born into just such conditions understood the complexities of local politics. They had extended kinship groups upon which they could call for help in emergencies and they brought invaluable skills to marriage with a European man, many of which were marriages of convenience. For European men in the fur trade, the frontier was devoid of opportunities for a domestic life unless they turned to aboriginal women. Single men lived in military-style barracks, their Spartan lives punctuated by periods of excessive drinking and dangerous voyages. A number of these marriages were essentially political. In a landscape where the dominant society was aboriginal, powerful chiefs and astute fur traders sought in an age-old fashion to cement alliances, formalize access and expand trading relationships through marriage. As a result, much of BC's non-Native and Native populations share common ancestries to an extent that many have either forgotten or prefer to repress.

For example, after British trader Robert Hunt's European wife died around 1850, he promptly married Ansnaq or Mary Ebbetts, granddaughter of Shakes, a chief who monopolized fur trade routes to the Interior on the Stikine River. Mary's mother, Chief of All Women, had been married to Abbitts, a Tlingit chief who controlled territory at the mouth of the Nass River. These women were typical in that they brought to their marriages the political weight of their rank and the prestige of family ties in a society that was deeply stratified with respect to class. Among Mary Ebbetts's possessions when she married, for example, was a Haida slave. It has been pointed out by historians that many European traders set aside their "country wives" once they were no longer useful in economic or political terms and then travelled east to formally marry European women. William Connolly, Amelia's father, was one who did.

Adele Perry, who delves into this complex social history in a brilliant piece of scholarship entitled *On the Edge of Empire: Gender, Race and the Making of British Columbia, 1849–1871*, provides evidence that attitudes toward First Nations, and particularly aboriginal women, became an expression of racist prejudice largely following the influx of British and American settlers. The

Americans brought the prejudices of their Indian wars and many of the British newcomers aspired to status denied them at home and seized the opportunity to bestow rank upon themselves. Stereotypes were born when they encountered the ruins of once rich and powerful societies demoralized by successive epidemics that had depopulated the landscape, shredded cultural legacies and shattered their economic underpinnings.

Yet many of these personal relationships were also based in genuine love and proved remarkably resilient and durable, as did the affectionate marriages of James and Amelia Douglas and Robert and Mary Ebbetts Hunt. Mary and Robert had 11 children. One daughter, Sarah Hunt, married Alexander Lyon and helped him found the city of Port Hardy on Vancouver Island in 1904. Another daughter, Annie Hunt, married Stephen Spencer, an American cannery operator at Alert Bay. They had seven children and moved to Victoria in 1900, becoming part of the social establishment. And a brother, George Hunt, became the chief assistant of famed anthropologist Franz Boas.

Few of these cross-cultural relationships, however, had the impact on BC's history that Amelia's marriage to James

Beaver woman and child in Fort St. John, 1904.
Glenbow Archives NA-494-25

Douglas was to have. In 1828, young James was temporarily in charge of Fort St. James when he apprehended a man wanted for the murder of two Hudson's Bay Company traders five years earlier at

The first citizen of Port Hardy

If rugged self-reliance was the watchword for frontier marriages, there are few better examples than that of Alexander Lyon and Sarah Hunt. They left the Hudson's Bay Company trading post at Fort Rupert by rowboat in 1904. The couple was bound for Hardy Bay in windswept Goletas Channel, about 30 kilometres north of present-day Port McNeill, along a wild and sparsely settled coast.

Alexander had taken a liking to the sheltered anchorage fed by the Quatse and Tsulquate rivers at the north end of Vancouver Island. The bay had been named by an equally admiring George Richards, captain of HMS *Plumper*, to commemorate Vice Admiral Thomas Masterman Hardy, who was captain of Lord Nelson's flagship HMS *Victory* at the Battle of Trafalgar in 1803.

Sarah was one of the tough, resilient daughters of Robert Hunt, who had been a fur trader at Fort Rupert for 20 years before buying the post outright in 1883, and Mary Ebbetts, a Tongass Tlingit woman from the North Coast. And

although Sarah was pregnant and approaching term, she didn't hesitate to accompany her husband on the long row to their new home. On landing, however, she slipped on the wet stones and went into premature labour. Alexander got her up into the one-room cabin he had built, then set out to get the nearest doctor from the Anglican mission in the village of Alert Bay, about 35 kilometres to the south.

Rowing like a demon, he made it as far as Fort Rupert when a storm blew up and drove him ashore with many kilometres of heavy seas still separating him from the doctor on Cormorant Island. His mother-in-law, however, called on her relatives in the emergency and a sea-going canoe sped him the rest of the way through heavy weather to get the doctor and then bring him back up the coast to Hardy Bay.

When Alexander and the doctor returned, they found Sarah lying on the floor of the cabin. She was exhausted but otherwise all right. Cradled in her arms was newborn Douglas Lyon, the first citizen of what would become Port Hardy, the commercial and industrial hub of northernmost Vancouver Island.

Fort George. Unfortunately, the suspect was killed when he tried to stab Douglas with an arrow. Even worse, the rash young clerk had gone into the house of the Carrier Chief Kwah to make the arrest. By violating the chief's prerogative to offer sanctuary he had caused the chief to lose face. Kwah seized the fort, overpowered Douglas and was preparing to kill him with a knife when Amelia intervened. She began throwing bales of recently arrived trade goods at the feet of the Carrier chief and his warriors. Kwah accepted them and, his honour satisfied, released his captive. Amelia's marriage to the hotheaded Douglas was to last 49 years and produce 13 children. She would have a private audience with Queen Victoria. And if her life ended in the tranquil obscurity she sought, it might also be argued that her legacy is the province itself, for without her

Lady Amelia Douglas and her family at their Victoria home. Aboriginal women understood local politics and brought invaluable skills to marriage with European men.
BC Archives G-03584

understanding of Kwah and her calm diplomatic solution, British Columbia might never have come to pass.

Opposite: Lady Douglas donned widow's weeds and withdrew from society after her husband's death.
BC Archives H-04909

5 Miners' Angels and Dance Hall Queens

A cold wind sighs through the evergreens. They cast deep, gloomy shadows across the old burying ground on the outskirts of Barkerville where weathered wooden headboards, time-darkened stone and rusty wrought iron straggle along the steep hillside. Almost 750 kilometres north of Greater Vancouver by road, this lonely little cemetery is where the luckless of Cameronton and Richfield staked their final claims—although by the 1880s those mining camps were gone, absorbed by Barkerville, the now-restored Cariboo boom town just up the road that is one of British Columbia's famous tourist destinations.

This old graveyard is one of BC's most important pioneer historic sites, for here lies the flotsam and jetsam of the gold rush in whose crucible of greed, brutality, courage and vision the province and its destiny were forged. And there are few more poignant reminders of the roles that women played in that grand adventure than the simple memorials raised to those who came in search of fortune and found only six feet of cold ground.

There is Jessie Heatherington, the "Scotch Lassie," debauched by a drunkard husband, abandoned and then murdered by an unknown assailant. And Marie Hageman, who probably came to work in the saloons, bestowing her favours for $1 a dance and a commission on every drink she could coax from a besotted miner. There's Margaret Blair, a much-loved wife who died giving birth to her fourth child at the desperately young age of 21. There's Isabella Hodgkinson, the camp washerwoman whose epitaph, "Sleep, Bella, Sleep," is her husband's bittersweet farewell to the wife who rose every day before dawn. And there is Janet Allen, "Big Jennie," the saloonkeeper who "dressed like a man, drank like a man and died like a man" in a carriage crash but for whom

Alturas Gold Mining Co. in Stout's Gulch, near Barkerville, circa 1868, by photographer Frederick Dally.
BC Archives A-04919

Dance hall girls, circa 1900. They bestowed their favours for $1 a dance and a commission on every drink they could coax besotted miners to buy.
Glenbow Archives NA-3439-3, NA-3439-2 and NA-3439-1

every flag flew at half-mast and who was eulogized in the *Cariboo Sentinel* as "nurse and friend to the miner" for her kindness toward the sick, injured or distressed.

These women were among the remarkable few carried by the gold-crazed tide of humanity that flooded up the Fraser River in 1858, spilled along its tributaries and seeped across the mountain passes, opening the remote and barely known regions of the Chilcotin, the Cariboo, the Kootenays and the Cassiar to European settlement. They came by steamboat and pack train from California, like Nellie Cashman. Born in Ireland the year before the great famine, she later immigrated to Boston, followed the California gold rush to San Francisco and then went on to BC, where she ran boarding houses and restaurants. The "Angel of the Cassiar" was legendary for her good works with the poor, the sick and the indigent. Although Nellie never

married—"Why child, I haven't had time for marriage. Men are a nuisance anyhow, now aren't they? They're just boys grown up," she told an American reporter—when her sister Fannie died, she raised five nieces and nephews. Yet the Angel was as tough as any sourdough. In 1874, she and six men packed more than a tonne of fresh supplies through deep snow to Dease Lake to avert an outbreak of scurvy and at the age of 78 she mushed a dog team 750 kilometres in Alaska. She died of pneumonia in Victoria in 1925 and is buried in Ross Bay Cemetery with the Sisters of St. Ann where her gravestone reads: "Friend of the sick and the hungry and to all men. Heroic apostolate of service among the western and northern frontier miners. Miner's Angel."

Others, no less tough than Nellie Cashman, came overland from the Prairies, struggling from valley to valley. The most famous of these was Catherine Schubert, born in Ireland in 1835. Four months pregnant, with three children

Nellie Cashman, circa 1874: The "Angel of the Cassiar" ran boarding houses and cared for the sick.
BC Archives D-01775

aged one, three and five in tow, she and her husband Augustus set out for the Cariboo from Fort Garry in 1862 with a

party of gold seekers later known as the "Overlanders." It was a perilous journey beset by hardships. Two drowned and the rest almost starved. But Catherine survived and while travelling down the Thompson River by raft she went into labour. She was cared for by the women of a First Nations settlement and her baby girl, Rose, was the first non-aboriginal citizen to be born in BC.

The catalyst for all these adventures—and more—can be traced to February 1858, when James Douglas delivered 800 ounces of gold dust from the Thompson River to the Hudson's Bay Company. When that gold was refined at a San Francisco mint, prospectors who had played out their diggings or had bad luck in California drifted north. On April 25, 1858, the American ship *Commodore* arrived at Fort Victoria, population less

"That was almost heaven. . ."

I used to waken in the morning to the sound of rushing Williams Creek and the song of the anvil from the O'Neil blacksmith's shop across the street and the sound of Billy Hodgkinson's pack horse with a bell carrying milk up town from the milk ranch down the road.

Another cheery sound was the water dripping into the water barrel in the wood shed. This had to be brought from the springs on the hillside in overhead wooden troughs and to the backs of the various homes by smaller troughs. Can't you hear the arguments and tempers rising on wash day when the first house took more than its share of the precious water?

On the cold, cold days the sound of the frost and snow crackled beneath our feet and the sidewalks as we ran home from school for our lunches. On those bitter days mother usually had a big pot of hot pea soup on the stove in the front room. Most of the house had to be closed off to keep us warm.

I recall the anxiety lest the snow should not have gone by May 24th so that we girls might wear our summer dresses for the usual picnic at Joe Mason's meadows up at Jack O'Clubs Lake.

Lottie Mabel Bowron and company enjoying a sleigh ride. Lottie was born in Barkerville in 1879 and became inspector of social welfare for about 800 female teachers, most of whom worked in rural one-room schools.
BC Archives C-09760

And then the lovely walks with Mother up to Richfield, through Chinatown, past Stout's Gulch and the canyon, where Billy Barker sank his shaft. The walk was to bring my father home. His office was in the old courthouse. . .

The exciting arrival of the stage on Thursday evening and its departure Saturday morning—everyone was excited when the stage came in—the children watched for it behind the church—then the cry being carried from one child to another—"Here, here's the stage, here's the stage."

If you've never travelled by the "BX" Barnard's Express then you've never travelled. Four days from here to Ashcroft—the lovely, spirited horses, the heavy red coaches. And to get to sit next to the driver on the box—that was almost heaven.

—Lottie Bowron, a native of Barkerville whose father, John Bowron, was an Overlander, quoted in *Barkerville: A Gold Rush Experience*, by Richard Thomas Wright

Ann and Rose Williams wash dishes at the Nettie L. mine in Ferguson in the Kootenays. Opportunities for women to work for wages were limited.
Mattie Gunterman Photo Vancouver Public Library VPL 2266

than 300, carrying 450 passengers bound for the goldfields. By the end of August, 1858, 20,000 people had arrived in Victoria and another 13,000 were moving into the Lower Mainland from the American side of the 49th parallel. In 1858, those miners took 106,000 ounces of gold from the Fraser River system, an amount worth more than $50 million at today's prices and a discovery of mind-boggling richness for its time.

It was essentially a male invasion—by 1861, there were still only 192 non-Native women living on the mainland, an area the size of Western Europe—and

The Flynn brothers and their wives at the Williams gold claim at Mosquito Creek in the Cariboo, 1903.
BC Archives A-03838

this distorted demographic resulted in what historian Adele Perry describes as an intensely homosocial culture. It was a society, she says, that continued to circumscribe women's lives in traditional ways. In an economy dominated by resource extraction and back-breaking labour, women's opportunities to work for wages were severely limited. A few entrepreneurs found themselves in business running laundries, boarding houses, saloons, bakeries and eating establishments or making clothes. Others took positions as governesses or teaching in public schools for pitifully small salaries that encouraged them to marry as quickly as the opportunity arose. Some were recruited as "hurdy-gurdies" who nominally provided dances and socializing for a fee but were often forced to provide sexual services on the side, although more than a few wound up married to former clients.

For all but the establishment elite in Victoria, life was hard, dangerous and unforgiving, as the grave markers at Barkerville attest. And yet, by the time these women were laid to rest, the social and demographic landscape of BC had been utterly transformed and a new province had been born, phoenix-like, amid the ashes of their endeavours.

The Hotel de France in Barkerville, circa 1863. Life was hard, dangerous and unforgiving, as the grave markers in the town attest.
BC Archives A-02051

German dancing girls, known as hurdy-gurdies, Barkerville, 1865. They provided dances for a fee, but often were forced into sex.
BC Archives G-00817

"Brought to America by some speculating, conscienceless scoundrel . . ."

Hurdy-Gurdy damsels are unsophisticated maidens of Dutch extraction, from "poor but honest parents" and morally speaking, they really are not what they are generally put down for. They are generally brought to America by some speculating, conscienceless scoundrel of a being commonly called a "Boss Hurdy." This man binds them in his service until he has received about a thousand per cent for his outlay. The girls receive a few lessons in the terpsichorean art, are put into a kind of uniform, generally consisting of a red waist, cotton print skirt and a half mourning headdress resembling somewhat in shape the topknot of a male turkey, this uniform gives them quite a grotesque appearance. Few of them speak English, but they soon pick up a few popular vulgarisms; if you bid one of them good morning your answer will likely be "itsh sphlaid out" or "you bet your life.

The Hurdy style of dancing differs from all other schools. If you ever saw a ring of bells in motion, you have seen the exact positions these young ladies are put through during their dance, the more muscular the partner, the nearer the approximation of the ladies' pedal extremities to the ceiling, and the gent who can hoist his "gal" the highest is considered the best dancer; the poor girls as a general thing earn their money very hardly.

—letter to the *Cariboo Sentinel*, September 6, 1866 (quoted in *British Columbia: A Centennial Anthology* edited by Reginald Eyre Watters)

6 Homesteads and Hard Women

Some languid evenings, when the late autumn light slants into the grasslands where the Nicola River tumbles toward the great, green glint of the Thompson at Spence's Bridge, everything seems burnished with gold, just as it must have appeared almost 120 years ago to homesteader Jessie Ann Smith. She'd come from her Scottish village as a bride in 1884, one of the multitude pulled into the unmapped interior of a remote and little-known colony on the far side of the world by a gold rush that began in 1858 and continued into the 20th century.

If raw gold is what prospectors sought in the Fraser Canyon, flooding up the two forks of the Thompson, up the Bonaparte and over the dry ridges into the Tulameen and the Similkameen valleys, some travellers looked on the land and saw wealth of another kind in the bunch grass and the dark loam of the creek bottoms. Boom towns like Barkerville, Fairview and Camp McKinney had to be fed and their hunger meant instant markets. Markets meant opportunities for producers. The gold rush launched a demand-driven expansion in frontier ranching and farming that lasted until World War I. Unlike the chic, sophisticated, urbanized province of today, 100 years ago 80 percent of BC's population lived rural lives under conditions that most city dwellers have difficulty imagining. There was no electricity, no telephones, no television or radio, no libraries. Schools, where they existed, were one-room affairs and children travelled far to attend. Few homesteads had running

Left: Children watch a pot suspended over a fire in the Windermere Valley in the East Kootenay. Glenbow Archives NA-1135-55

Right: Jessie Ann Smith in her wedding dress. Her legendary apples, winners of gold and silver medals in the US and Canada, were fit for a king. Photo courtesy Nicola Valley Museum Archives Association PF 913

Maria Rosalia Marciana Blount was born and raised in Gibraltar. She married Captain George Pittendrigh and sailed around the Horn arriving in New Westminster in 1874. City of Richmond Archives photo no. 1978 2 6

water and the only source of heat was the wood stove. Transportation was on foot, on horseback or by rowboat and save for a few non-perishable staples, households were expected to produce their own food. And, without doctors or hospitals, women were expected to give birth at home.

Pioneer rancher, world-renowned fruit farmer, wife, widow and tenacious single mother, Jessie Ann Smith rode that astonishing wave for more than 60 years, a small yet symbolic player in the great game of empire—although her charming autobiography, *Widow Smith of Spence's Bridge*, deftly edited and published by Murphy Shewchuk of Merritt in 1989, reveals it is doubtful she held

that perception of herself.

While the mining camps were characterized by their transience, farming required families to put down roots—for generations in the case of orchardists. And in contrast to the almost exclusively male society of the gold creeks, farms desperately needed women and children if they were to function effectively as economic units. Farms also secured territorial rights. The mining camps were full of bellicose American adventurers and the British authorities understood that to secure their colonial hold, the land had to be occupied and made productive. To persuade men to settle required the society of women; achieving imperial ambitions required white women. But in 1861, there were fewer than 100 European women in BC for

Clearing land in Beaton, near Revelstoke, circa 1900. Mattie Gunterman Photo Vancouver Public Library VPL 2319

Drawing by Emily Carr entitled *The Women Tell Her of Such Woes As How The Wind Won't Dry The Clothes.* BC Archives PDP05894

"Drudgery so awful. . ."

For women in the rural and frontier regions maintaining a home offered few challenges as horrific as the weekly laundry.

Monday was considered "Wash Day."

Beginning early in the morning water had to be brought from its source, often a creek or well. As many as 200 litres might be necessary for the family wash—water that had to be boiled over whatever heat source was available.

Homemade lye soap, so hard on the hands, rubbed skin raw as women separated the items by color and fragility, scrubbed and scoured, sometimes over several changes of boiling water. Rinsing several times was often necessary. Then the laundry had to dry, usually outside no matter what the weather.

The process lasted well into the evening. Husbands were accustomed to cold dinners on Mondays.

Tuesday meant ironing. This was another challenge since irons also had to be heated. The "sad iron" was a succession of hot irons which were heated to replace those that had cooled. Each iron weighed between seven and eight pounds but some weighed up to 14.

This drudgery was so awful that even women of lower income would scrounge together funds to hire washerwomen. A woman of higher income would use a commercial laundry. Destitute women who took in laundry could do it at their own home and at their own pace.

Washing machines and electricity ended the pioneer's curse.

—exhibit notes, Clallam County Museum, Port Angeles, Washington

every 1,000 men. The first effort to redress this imbalance involved the free transportation of wives with the Royal Engineers to New Westminster and the promise of 150 acres of free land for each soldier or his widow who stayed in the new colony. The offer of a quarter section of land to homesteaders prepared to clear and "improve" the property was a compelling incentive.

Yet the demand for women who would transform a fur trade and gold rush culture into a settler society soon took a more exotic form. In 1862, the first of what became known as the "Bride Ships" began arriving at Fort Victoria loaded with young single women

First ranchers in the Elk Valley, 1905. Back row, from left: Joe Fristal (pointed hat, gunbelt, long gun); Elizabeth Musel; Anna Kiasner (striped blouse); Harry Kiasner Sr. (white shirt, pipe, soft cap); Emil Fristal. Front row: Phil Musel Sr. (little girl's head on his knee); Phil Musel's daughter Emily Musel; Anna Fristal (white pompom necklace); John Fristal (bowler hat, large gun); Jerry Kiasner; Millie Fristal (with mandolin); Harry Kiasner Jr. (little boy in front with gun in his lap). Glenbow Archives NA-1320-4

recruited in Britain. One sailing ship, *The Seaman's Bride*, put in at San Francisco after a Pacific crossing from Australia only to have the women "stolen" by American gallants and married before the vessel could leave again for BC, much to the fury of *British Colonist* editor and future premier Amor de Cosmos. When the *Tynemouth* arrived at Fort Victoria that September with 59

An early farmhouse in Richmond, circa 1908.
City of Richmond Archives photo
no. 1984 17 71

women aboard, the town went into a near frenzy. Royal Marines and Royal Navy bluejackets had to be mustered to permit the passengers to walk from the docks to their accommodation.

The youngest—some were orphans as young as 12—were found positions as domestic servants until they were of an age to marry. The eldest found positions as teachers and governesses. Those who could marry frequently did so quickly, some the same day they

arrived. Few of these women and those who followed had the faintest idea of the hardship, loneliness and privation they faced beyond the bustling little fort. Land had to be cleared, preserves put up for the long winter, living conditions were primitive, husbands were often away for long periods, babies were often born with little more than the assistance of neighbours. In addition, pioneer women faced the challenging task of keeping clean not only the bed and table linens but a bewildering array of crinolines, camisoles, petticoats, pantaloons, corsets, gloves, stockings and the white lace dresses required for fashionable summer wear. Some, even those who came long after the Bride

Ships had ceased, found only heartbreak and despair, turning to suicide or abandoning families. Yet many more women found satisfying futures in the new colony. Vancouver teacher Peter Johnson's book *Voyages of Hope: The Saga of the Bride-Ships* traces the bountiful,

Mr. and Mrs. W.H. Grassie stand next to a felled tree on Georgia Street in Vancouver around 1886, the year the city was incorporated.
Charles S. Bailey photo, City of Vancouver Archives CVA SGN 152

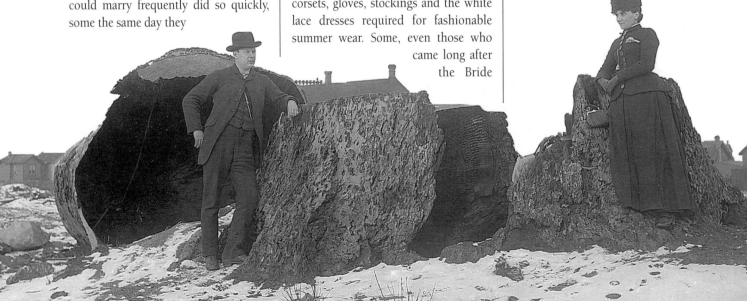

richly fulfilled lives of a number of them.

The Bride Ships were one extreme of a trend that would see the number of non-Native women in BC increase by 1,500 percent over the next decade. The majority however, came by more conventional means, often accompanied by husbands and children. One of them was Jessie Ann Smith. In 1858, just as authority was passing from the Hudson's Bay Company to the newly minted colony of British Columbia in a muddy yard at Fort Langley, she was six and sitting in her first class in Scotland, where her father was a comfortable member of the upper middle class. Twenty-eight years later, with a toddler and a baby, she was moving into a four-room log cabin on a half section homestead 30 kilometres beyond the end of the road. The ranch was four days' ride from the nearest store. She'd already seen grizzlies, cougars, wolves and black bears in the valley and lay awake her first nights trembling with fear.

"The wild grass was abundant and grew shoulder high. John bought a few cows, two horses and some pigs and I raised chickens," she wrote later. "We made butter for sale and traded butter, eggs and pork at Mr. Carrington's store at Nicola Lake and the store at Coutlee." Ten years later, the family was raising fruit at Spence's Bridge. When her husband died, she kept the fruit farm going.

Her apples were legendary and won many gold and silver medals for the British Empire and in the United States and Canada. Her moment of fame came in 1909 when King Edward VII insisted on seeing her gold medal entry of Grimes Golden Apples at the Royal Horticultural Society Exhibition in London. The exhibit had been misplaced and the king was not amused. "The apples which I have come to see are those of the Widow Smith of Spence's Bridge," her autobiography recounts. She died at the age of 93 in 1946 and was buried beside the husband she had outlived by more than 40 years.

If the gold rush had unleashed political, economic and ideological forces that transformed the landscape, women like

Mrs. Chancy Smith milks a cow on her Elk Valley farm in the East Kootenay. W. Bovin and Chancy Smith are in the background.
Glenbow Archives NA-1320-5

Widow Smith and the girls of the Bride Ships came to domesticate transient males who were more interested in striking it rich and moving on. Pioneer women who fashioned a permanent home in the wilderness and encouraged those men to settle down were ultimately to prove more significant in the making of what was to become British Columbia than the men that history usually credits.

7 The Search for Eden

A sudden, cold slant of rain spatters across the glossy leaves of salal with a brisk, plastic rustle. The wind picks up, hissing and roaring through the high canopy. One more weather front is moving in across San Josef Bay toward the bleak northern tip of Vancouver Island. Blows like this were lethal in the days of sail. The brig *Consort* was wrecked in San Josef Bay in 1860. The *Henry Denis* and the *Hermit* were both lost here within days of one another in 1892, the schooner *Wanderer* sank in 1896, the *Hilmeny* in 1906 and the *Suzie M. Plummer* foundered with all hands in 1910.

Yet at Cape Scott, just northwest of here, hardy Danish settlers sought to establish a farming and fishing colony in 1897. They were inspired by similar settlements of Norwegian immigrants at Quatsino Sound and Bella Coola and served in their own right as an inspiration for Finns settling at Sointula on Malcolm Island in 1901.

Explore the dripping, moss-muffled woods up here, a good hike beyond the end of the Island Highway, and you'll find the assorted bric-a-brac of long-vanished human habitation. There are faint signs of the ancient Lalasiquala village of Nomch, abandoned before Europeans arrived. And more obvious evidence of those long-departed newcomers: a rusting bed frame, stray buttons lost between the floorboards of a post office rotting back into the forest floor, log rounds corduroyed into boggy ground, the trails leading off to unseen destinations in the gloom.

Ever since James Douglas looked on the flower-laced meadows and Garry oaks of south Vancouver Island and declared he was building the new Hudson's Bay Company fort in "a perfect Eden," it's been said of British Columbia that two kinds of people sought to lose

Men carved clearings from the forest but women built communities, like these early Norwegian settlers on BC's coast.
BC Central Coast Archives

Group from the home for girls at Port Simpson, 1890s. The home was run from 1893 to the 1920s.
BC Archives B-08046

themselves in its wilderness: those wanting to play God and those wanting to hide from God. A third group might be added: those wanting to re-create that same Eden that momentarily blossomed in the mind of the future governor when he looked on the blue brocade of camas blooms spread across rippling fields of grass under spring sunshine.

Few statements of that intent are quite as explicit as "The Cape Scott Song," a homegrown saga of the time about the paradise in which the settlers proclaim that "slowly we will here an Eden make."

So this place, still at the far fringe of human habitation in Canada's third-largest province, seems a good spot to contemplate the often nameless and frequently overlooked women who put up with privation, loneliness and isolation in helping efforts to create Heaven on Earth, or at least to assist earthly sinners to find a way of climbing more easily to the metaphysical realm.

Since the early days of the colony, BC has been a blast furnace of missionary zeal, of fervent searches for Utopia and of a series of experiments in social engineering in the name of God, whose consequences—both uplifting and destructive—the province is still trying to sort out here on Earth. Christians from the Roman Catholic, Anglican and other Protestant faiths perceived the landscape west of the Rockies as a country filled with pagans, heathens, wicked men and fallen women requiring the ministrations of salvation. Others—from Finnish freethinkers on the West Coast to Doukhobors fleeing Russian persecution into the mountain valleys of the Kootenays—saw, in a wilderness they perceived as uninhabited, the possibility

"How to knit a sock. . ."

She would be alone for months at a time, with nothing but the Indian women up there. They were Nishga Indians, so Robert, my husband, as a boy learned the Nishga language and could rattle it off before he could talk English, because they had girls in the house working for them so Grandma could teach the girls how to do things. She had never done much sewing herself because they were pretty well protected. They came from Ireland and they belonged to the gentry in Ireland and moved over here. So she'd never done much housework and she'd never knitted in her life. But now she had to teach the Indians how to knit a sock.

The only way she could learn how to knit a sock was to unravel a sock that was made by a machine. The heels are turned entirely differently than a homemade sock. So she and my father-in-law figured out how these socks were made, and so they taught the Indians how to knit. So the Indians up the Skeena and on the Nass knit their socks with the heels the same way as the boughten socks, which comes in from the side. The homemade comes square up. And, of course, they had to make their own candles; they had to do a lot of things that she had never done in her life.

—Mrs. Robert Tomlinson, daughter-in-law of Alice Tomlinson, a missionary in the Nass Valley in the 1870s

Doukhobor women serve a meal to men workers. They saw, in the wilderness, the possibility of their own redemption.
BC Archives C-01356

of their own redemption in founding and perfecting communities of the like-minded at a remove from the corrupting temptations of the secular world. Women have played significant roles in all of these organizations as willing participants, unwitting victims or well-meaning perpetrators. Their sometimes central participation has tended to be overlooked because the deep-rooted social values and assumptions of their

time pushed them from the rugged foreground reserved for men into the comforting background of romantic stereotypes and expectations.

For example, the first woman to arrive at Sointula, the Finnish Utopian settlement launched about 300 kilometres northwest of Vancouver, was the newly married Anna Wilander. This young woman from New York proved crucial to the establishment of the colony, cooking and washing for 14 men and bringing them hot food in the winter bush while they furiously cleared land and built shelter for the families and 15 children who would follow. Sointula was founded on principles of women's equality. Founder Matti Kurikka was a student of Minna Canth, a leading Finnish suffragette. At a time when they were denied the vote and even status as persons in mainstream society, women at Sointula held their own meetings to determine their role in

Missionaries brought more than new religious beliefs, they brought new fashions for these young Muchalat women. BC Archives I-31553

"We crawled. . ."

We landed at Clayton's store [in 1894]. There was about 40 of us, mostly women and children and two or three men. I can picture them leaving Clayton's. They all had packs on. My father had my blanket, I had my suitcase, and the little children were riding on top of the packs on the men, and there was a long string of us went up. The trail was narrow, crooked. We crawled on trees across the creeks; especially we had to cross a big river, that they call Nusatsum; it [the bridge] was just poles and my father led me across. We all got as far as what we call Hagensborg now. My uncle, Ole Gaarden, lived this side of Snootli Creek and we stayed at his place.
—Annie Engebretson, among the first at the Norwegian settlement in Bella Coola
BC Archives tape 4032:1 Sound Heritage Series

the community. (They created a day care facility so that women were free to work, although it proved less successful than planned when those committed to the ideal decided to stay home when it came to their own babies and toddlers.) Even in Utopia the growing self-determination of the women created fault lines. Some men resented their autonomy as derailing the male vision of a perfect community. Perhaps as a result, Anna is reduced to the merest footnote in the official narratives. Of two recent histories, one doesn't mention her and the other identifies her only as Mrs. Wilander, effectively defining her as an extension of her husband's persona.

Indeed, across the contemporary historic record, female missionaries are often seen largely as helpmates, submerged in their husbands' valiant strife in a war for souls. The humdrum work of nuns as nursing and teaching sisters is eclipsed by the illustrious work of conversion by priests and bishops. And yet, agree with their objectives or not, the social impact of these women was significant. The provincial archives are rife

Sister Mary Providence was 22 years old when she arrived in Victoria in 1859 to join the first four Sisters of St. Ann as their Superior.
BC Archives A-02419

with photos of aboriginal women abandoning their traditional dress for Victorian corsets and taking up the new feminine labours of weaving, spinning and sewing that were introduced by missionary wives.

The group of missionary women that was to have the most profound influence

came from Montreal. Salome Valois, Angele Gauthier, Virginie Brassard and Mary Lane answered a plea from Bishop Modeste Demers for teachers at a school for girls in Fort Victoria. These four members of the Sisters of St. Ann—a religious order founded in Montreal in 1850—had taken the veil as Sister Marie du Sacré-Coeur, Sister Marie Angèle, Sister Marie-Luména and Sister Marie-de-la-Concepcion. They arrived in Fort Victoria on June 5, 1858, took residence in a vermin-infested hut with dirt floors in the midst of a gold rush and had St. Ann's School for Young Ladies up and running in less than three weeks.

Enrolled were Hélène Lavoie, Emma and Henriette Yates, Emélie Morel, Emélia Desmarais, Elizabeth Dodd, Elizabeth Anderson, recently arrived from India, Virginia Gurta and Lucy Angèle. And six years later, at a time when advanced education was not thought particularly necessary for future

Schoolgirls, nuns and school officials gather for a Passion Play at St. Mary's Church in Mission, circa 1894.
City of Vancouver Archives CVA LGN 579

wives and mothers, the *British Colonist* newspaper was noting that the results of examinations in natural philosophy, English grammar, modern and ancient history, geography and mythology were a testament to the girls' teachers from Quebec. By 1870, the sisters had established a convent and later St. Ann's Academy, which was expanded to provide commercial studies for young women in 1913. Although the academy closed in 1973, the nuns continued at Queenswood House of Studies, where they offered retreats for prayer, study and contemplation. They also provided a chapel for University of Victoria students and remained active in ministries concerned with social justice, rehabilitation, prison work and care for the sick and the elderly.

The nuns serve to remind us that while buildings may tumble and the forest reclaim scores of failed Utopian dreams from Cape Scott to Creston, much important spiritual work was done in the service of those dreams by unrecognized and under-appreciated women. Their vital legacy endures and continues to shape the social and cultural fabric of the province they helped bring into the world.

Four girls at the Coqualeetza residential school in Sardis, which was established by the Methodist Church in 1888. BC Archives I-51769

"A right to speak at meetings. . ."

We arrived here late at night. It was pitch-black and all the bay was covered with these big kelps—these great big snakes in the water with these great big heads on them. The boat tied up to some sort of a slip and we had to walk along these logs to the shore where this little shack was.

In this log cabin were five double bunks for all these families. Hay was piled high on these bunks for a mattress and my husband and I and two children got one of these bunks for our own.

They were going to share everything. Everyone would be working for the common good. No one owned anything separately and individually. They planned to farm and log and all the proceeds would be divided equally.

I think the main idea was to have a free society. Especially, they emphasized that women should have equal rights with men. At that time, women had no property rights, they had

no rights whatsoever in wages, so this was one thing that applied here. The women had a-dollar-a-day wages, as the men did, and they had a right to speak at meetings and they had a right to vote. And they had to work. Everyone had to work.

Another thing they wanted was a society where there would be no government church. There would be no liquor vending and no women would have to sell themselves. . . They could have religion, but no one would be forcing any particular religion and anyone could believe as they wished. The company was to look after the children—all the expenses, clothing, food and schooling. No one would be charged extra for children. The idea was that later on the children would be the workers and they would look after the elders. All the women went to work in the kitchen or laundry or wherever they were needed and they had a nursery where their children were sent.

—Kaisa Raisman, arrived at Sointula, aged 22, on June 3, 1902
BC Archives tape 4032:1 Sound Heritage Series

8 Women at Work

Except for the ruin of a stone chimney under blackberry brambles and fading memories in the surrounding community, little remains of the Hudson's Bay Company outpost at Fort Rupert where British Columbia's formal labour history began. It was here, in 1850, that the wives of eight Scottish coal miners brought in to work a seam for the company prodded their husbands to stand up for their rights, prompting the first job action in BC.

The miners and their families had been enticed to make the dangerous journey around Cape Horn with promises of steady work and daily rations of beef, mutton, beer, grog and new wine. Once they arrived, however, they

Women and children behind a marching band leading a United Mine Workers of America parade in 1913 during the Big Strike, which paralyzed Vancouver Island coalfields between 1912 and World War I.
BC Archives E-02631

Anne Muir and her coal miner husband, John, came to Fort Rupert where in 1850 harsh conditions triggered BC's first serious labour dispute.
BC Archives E-02392

"Cautioned by their menfolk. . ."

I note that the wives of the miners are the most outspoken and bitterest of enemies to the soldiers. They are often cautioned by their men folks when speaking in reckless tones of the soldiers.

—Undercover Pinkerton agent's report from Nanaimo during The Big Strike of 1912 (quoted in *Boss Whistle: The Coal Miners of Vancouver Island Remember* by Lynn Bowen, Nanaimo and District Museum and Rocky Point Books, revised edition, 2002)

When the miners decided they'd rather move their families to California and take their chances in the goldfields, the company had the men thrown in irons. The captain of the trading ship *England*, which was standing off the fort, was instructed to refuse passage for their families. The women were having none of that. They gathered their children, defied the company's authority and boldly swept aboard the ship, refusing to be dislodged. Annie later settled at Sooke where the Muirs proved one of the most industrious pioneer families in BC history.

Women like those who came to Fort Rupert more than 150 years ago were no strangers to work, of course. Nor were

discovered that things weren't quite as the company had promised. Housing was wretched, they were expected to live off the land because the company could make more money exporting the beef and mutton from its farms at Fort Victoria. (The workers were assured they'd soon come to prefer "wild food.")

Their tools weren't suitable, the coal seam proved to be only a hand's span in thickness and the miners, who prided themselves as professionals, were expected to work as common labourers. To make things worse, no sooner had the wives and children landed than a 16-canoe Kwagiut war party hauled up on the beach, erected 16 poles and placed a human head—trophies from their raid on the south coast—on each one. Annie Muir, wife of the mining contingent's leader John Muir, was offered her choice of any two heads. She was not amused.

Along with the gospels, missionaries brought new technologies to the North Coast, like these spinning wheels.
BC Archives B-03573

Our First Teacher.

Miss Georgia Sweney, a "voice in the wilderness" who, in a land of virgin forest, instituted teaching at our first public school at Hastings Sawmill on primeval Burrard Inlet, 1872, now Vancouver. An accomplish'd musician, a skilled artist, she could also milk a cow. Portrait presented, 1941, by her daughter Esther Cummings, Santa Paula. City Archives J5th

Miss Georgia Sweney, the first teacher at Vancouver's first public school at Hastings Sawmill, 1872. City of Vancouver Archives CVA PORT P556N235

"She rules through the affections. . ."

Female teachers, as a rule, possess greater aptitude for communicating knowledge, and are usually better disciplinarians, especially among young children, than males. Woman's mission is pre-eminently that of an educator. Her softening, refining, and elevating influence contributes largely to the success in the classroom. Patient and painstaking, she rules through the affections, her authority being thus based upon love, this trait of character is reciprocated by those with whom she comes in contact.

—John Jessop, *Second Annual Report on Public Schools*, (quoted in *Their Own History: Women's Contribution to the Labour Movement of British Columbia* by Betty Griffin and Susan Lockhart, United Fishermen and Allied Workers' Union/CAW Seniors Club, 2002)

the women who already occupied the landscape. Helen Meilleur, whose poignant memoir of Fort Simpson, *A Pour of Rain*, opens a window on the lives lived in and around the coastal fur trade forts, recounts the burden of being a wife in that male-dominated society. "She loaded and unloaded his canoe, cleaned the fish he caught, skinned the animals he trapped, made gear and clothing and mats and baskets she carried," Meilleur wrote of one aboriginal woman she observed as a girl. "She carried home firewood from distances of two miles; she carried baskets and cedar mat rolls full of possessions and cedar boxes full of food," she noted of her childhood observations at the dawn of the last century.

First Nations women were a crucial part of the work force, whether using the old technologies of cedar bark baskets and digging sticks or the new ones brought from Europe and Asia. Glenbow Archives NA-1700-80

And yet, perhaps the perception that things were harder for aboriginal women than they were for the wives of Europeans of the period reflects a cultural bias. Scholar James Axtell, in his study *Natives and Newcomers: The Cultural Origins of North America*, notes that one of the repressed social problems of the colonial period was that many "white" women captured or rescued by Natives came to prefer their new life and resisted

Native cannery workers on Cormorant Island, about three kilometres off the northeast coast of Vancouver Island, early 1900s.
BC Archives E-07419

returning to so-called civilization. "The great majority of white Indians left no explanation for their choice," he writes. "Forgetting their original language and their past, they simply disappeared into their adopted society. But those captives who returned to write narratives of their experiences left several clues to the motives of those who chose to stay behind.

"They stayed because they found Indian life to possess a strong sense of community, abundant love, and uncommon integrity—values the English colonists also honored, if less successfully. But Indian life was attractive for other values—for social equality, mobility, adventure and, as two adult converts acknowledged, 'the most perfect freedom, the ease of living and the absence of those cares and corroding solicitudes which so often prevail with us'."

It can also be argued that the crucial

moment in 1850 when some strong Scottish women at Fort Rupert defied the powerful Hudson's Bay Company marked a sea change in the role of women at work for both Natives and non-Natives. Pioneer women of all ethnic backgrounds ran ranches, carried the mail, bore children in the bush, hauled freight and shot game for the table as a

matter of course, but by 1911 more than 6,000 women in BC—about one in five—had made the transition from subsistence economics to the wage economy and formally entered the workforce. This

Telephone switchboard and operators at British Columbia Telephones Ltd. in 1898. Dominion Photo Company, Vancouver Public Library VPL 23795

shift in labour and economics proved to be the early harbinger of a series of changes, later accelerated by two world wars, that would utterly change the structure of British Columbian society and women's roles in it.

For Native women, the transition began when their labour became the assembly-line engine of the fish-processing business in canneries that sought to exploit huge salmon runs returning to remote rivers on the wild coast. At the time, these women were at the cutting edge of technology and mechanization. "Native women cleaned fish and filled cans amid clanking tinning machines, alongside steam vats and tray boilers, near conveyor and transmission belts, amid steam, and pipes, and foremen," observes Rolf Knight in *Indians at Work: An Informal History of Native Labour in British Columbia, 1858–1930.* "Those canneries may seem primitive by today's standards, but they were the industrialism of the resource frontier." Non-Native women were not far behind. Japanese,

Teacher Dorothy Alison and her class at the Model School in Vancouver, 1907. C. Bradbury photo, City of Vancouver Archives CVA SGN 1586

Chinese and European women soon moved into the canneries, too, part of a multicultural mosaic that those ignorant of history have come to believe a recent phenomenon.

And the expansion of urban life around seats of government, seaports and resource industries created demand for domestic servants, nurses, teachers

"A storm-tossed ship with a group of drunken miners. . ."

Mabel Blake came to Vancouver in 1913 armed with an English teaching certificate but had to wait until the following January before she found work at Minto on Vancouver Island. She had taught only a few days when a government replacement teacher arrived who had seniority over her. It was back to Vancouver on a storm-tossed ship with a group of drunken miners as fellow travellers. Another offer soon arrived, however, and she went off to Sand Creek School near Grand Forks, in the Kootenays. That fall she found herself in yet another school, this time in a Swedish logging community of five families at Hilltop, situated some 2,000 feet up from Fife, a whistle stop on the Kettle Valley Railway.

The schoolhouse was a square building with a large classroom in front, while the teacher's bedroom and kitchen were at the back. Mabel taught all grades, including one or two beginners who had to learn English first.

At her next posting in Bridesville, she had to ride a horse to get to the school, going down a steep bank to the creek below, riding through the creek, then up another bank to the road. It was while teaching there that she met young Juliet Bell, a deaf student who changed her career. In order to help Juliet, Mabel decided to investigate what government programs were available for deaf children. She discovered that classes for the deaf were being held in Vancouver; by the following fall she had joined the staff at what was to become Jericho Hill School.

—from *Women of British Columbia* by Jan Gould, Hancock House, 1975

and the light manufacturing of garments among women of European, Asian and aboriginal descent. Later, women occupied positions as telephone operators and retail clerks. Some scholars suggest these women received shabby treatment from a sexist union movement that perceived them as a threat to male prerogatives. Some unionists even lobbied for government restriction of female access to the labour market. However, in December 1911, the labour newspaper *The Federationist* was arguing vigorously against such short-sighted folly and in favour of giving women the franchise. "Women are going to get the ballot," the paper warned. "They will have power to wield and whether they use it wisely or not depends upon how we educate them."

Indeed, women persevered and continued to fight for the very unions that sought to shunt them into unskilled, low-paying job ghettos. One such ghetto was the teaching profession. But it was here that what proved to be among the most transformative developments for women took shape. In 1872, a new Public Schools Act replaced the moribund system begun by the Hudson's Bay Company. Two years later, almost half the teachers in BC were women and they took their ideas of equality to the most remote reaches of the province.

One of them was a spirited campaigner for equal rights for women who had been born in Victoria in 1863 and at the age of 27 became the first female high school teacher in BC. Four years later Agnes Deans Cameron was appointed the first female principal but was fired in 1906 for insisting that women deserved the same pay scales as men in the teaching profession. No quitter, she responded by working as a journalist and by trekking down the

Mackenzie River with her niece in 1908, becoming the first woman to reach the Arctic by an overland route. Her book about this trip (*The New North*, 1910) became a literary sensation. When Cameron died suddenly of complications following surgery for appendicitis in 1912, the *Victoria Daily Colonist* (May 14, 1912) described her as "the most remarkable woman citizen of the province." She was 48.

By 1909 the tough, resourceful and resilient pioneer women of Cameron's generation had organized themselves into the Women's Educational Club. Betty Griffin and Susan Lockhart point out in *Their Own History: Women's Contribution to the Labour Movement of*

Agnes Deans Cameron, at age 27 in 1890, was the first female high school teacher in BC, and soon the first female principal.
BC Archives F-08820

British Columbia that from an early initiative of that organization arose the powerful BC Teachers' Federation, a social and political institution that still has a profound influence on public policy almost a century later. And it all began in Fort Rupert, where the angry pioneer wives of a handful of ill-treated coal miners said "Enough," faced down the bullying of a powerful colonial employer and ignited a women's movement that is still active today.

9 Elite Excess & Riff-Raff Reality

If many pioneers came to early British Columbia in flight from the stifling conventions and social stratification of Europe, others came intent on establishing the same society in the colonies—but with themselves on top. So, less than a decade after the union of Vancouver Island with the mainland, the colony had developed its own Upstairs-Downstairs class structure. At one end of the spectrum was a genteel life of high teas, debutantes, calling cards and fancy balls for gowned ladies and gentlemen in glittering military attire. At the other were the brothels and dance halls where another class of woman tried to survive in a world without safety nets, in a world in which women were not considered legal persons and had few property rights.

The Victoria police chief's report for 1886 says that in addition to a cruel traffic in female slaves by Natives and 100 women working in Chinatown, there were four brothels in the downtown run by European madams employing 38 women. These brothels were licensed by the city as "dance halls." One long-standing rumour, wrote the late historian Terry Reksten, who cited the police report, held that a passage connected some of these establishments to the exclusive Union Club. Nevertheless, a local newspaper drew an editorial bead on the dance halls as "sinks of iniquity and pollution" where "prostitution and kindred vices, in all their hideous deformity and disease in every form, lurk."

That was Downstairs. Upstairs, "society" women like Julia Trutch, polished wife of Lieutenant-Governor Joseph Trutch, her brilliant sister Caroline O'Reilly, wife of the province's commissioner of both gold and Indian reserves, and the elegant Sarah Crease, wife of Judge Henry Pering Pellew Crease who drafted most of the new province's first laws, were creating their own hothouse culture in Victoria. The snobs of this arriviste establishment now felt comfortable snubbing the likes

Tea in the garden at Pentrelew, 1201 Fort St., Victoria, 1897. The four children of Frederick George Walker and Mary Maberley Crease with their aunt, Josephine Crease.
BC Archives F-06877

Left: Mae Field was a dance hall girl at Dawson. Women of the gold rush demimonde, the world of prostitutes, dance hall girls and entertainers who lived on the outskirts of respectable society, were a fiercely independent lot, defying post-Victorian society to travel north and endure incredible hardship, and sometimes heartbreak, as they, too, sought their fortunes.
© Canadian Museum of Civilization, negative no. J6215

Above left: The artist Josephine Crease (1890), daughter of Sarah and Henry Crease, the attorney general.
BC Archives F-06875
Above: Caroline Trutch married Peter O'Reilly and emerged as a bright, vivacious spirit of Victoria's high society, renowned for her singing abilities.
BC Archives G-09394

of Amelia Douglas. The former governor's Cree wife seemed to prefer her social eclipse and a life of relative seclusion from the new social whirl. Reading the racist attitudes toward Natives and the social bigotry revealed in the Trutch correspondence, one can understand why she might have enjoyed her own company rather more than that of the new establishment. Small wonder that Robert Melrose, a working-class fellow at Craigflower Farm, should note wryly in his diary (held in the collection of the Provincial Archives of BC): "Great Ball held at Victoria, riff-raff excluded."

Yet many of these newly arrived pioneer women came from Irish and Scottish families that were themselves excluded from England's upper crust by similar ethnic prejudice. In BC, they suddenly found themselves enriched by cheap land, the torrent of wealth flowing from the gold camps, coal mines, sawmills and ranches and the new markets this wealth created.

The evidence of a hunger for social status among the upwardly mobile middle class and the aspiring lesser gentry in exile is found both on the skyline of the capital's still exclusive Rocklands neighbourhood—and in the pretentious names settlers gave the new homes they carved from rain forest and rangeland. Joan Dunsmuir's husband, Robert, a coal baron who became BC's first millionaire and one of the wealthiest men in North America, built her a grandiose castle in Rocklands and named it "Craigdarroch." Captain Walter Colquhoun Grant built a great, curved carriage road to his log cabin at Sooke and named what visitors described as a shanty "Mullachard," after his ancestral home. Mary Ann Raby was living on a farm in Saanich when sailor

Diamond Lill Davenport, a dance hall girl of the gold-rush era.
Yukon Archives, Canadian Museum of Civilization Collection 3829

Downstairs

The Prostitutes: On the creek—nine in number—put on great airs. They dress in male attire and swagger through the saloons and mining camps with cigars or huge qwids of tobacco in their mouths, cursing and swearing and look like anything but the angels in petticoats heaven intended they should be.

Each has a revolver or bowie knife attached to her waist, and it is quite a common occurrence to see one or more women dressed in male attire playing poker in the saloons, or drinking whiskey at the bars. They are a degraded set, and all good men in the vicinity wish them hundreds of miles away.
—*Victoria Daily Colonist*, September 10, 1862, cited in *Barkerville* by Richard Thomas Wright, Winter Quarters Press, 1998

Left top: Lady Aberdeen, centre, settled on the Coldstream Ranch near Vernon in the Okanagan.
BC Archives A-01071

Left bottom: Victoria garden parties like this one on Rockland Avenue just weeks before the First World War began were often lavish and elegant affairs.
BC Archives A-02885

William Thompson found her so irresistible he jumped ship, proposed marriage and, when she accepted, cleared 400 hectares, bought 19 pigs and named his new estate "Bannockburn." There was a Fairfield and a Fintry, a Trebatha and a Roslyn, a Regent's Park and an Armadale, an Erin Hall and a Pentrelew, a Cary Castle and a Hatley Castle—the last also built by the Dunsmuir family with clear instructions to architect Samuel Maclure: "Money doesn't matter, just build what I want." G.P.V. and Helen Akrigg argue convincingly in their *British Columbia Chronicle* that it was deliberate British colonial policy to "recreate on Vancouver Island the social structure of England, a stalwart squirearchy with the working class properly relegated to an inferior station."

In addition to minor bureaucrats hoping to clamber up the colonial administration to acceptance in England, high society in Victoria was fuelled by an influx of second sons of landowners seeking their fortunes in the

Above: Craigdarroch Castle built by Robert Dunsmuir, BC's first millionaire.
Harbour Archives 3246

Below: Beautiful Kathleen O'Reilly, seen here with a friend.
BC Archives I-51791

colonies, well-connected junior officers of the Royal Navy and adventurous spirits from the aristocracy who saw the new province as a place to experiment with scientific agriculture. For example, Isabel Gordon, the Countess of Aberdeen, settled with her husband on the Coldstream Ranch near Vernon in the Okanagan. Winifred Ashburnam set out for a 200-hectare homestead on Cowichan Lake that her husband had purchased sight unseen. And a member of the Bowes-Lyons—that's the late Queen Mother's family—is said to have wound up teaching music at Cowichan

Station following an ill-starred love affair that earned disapproval at home. An urban gentry flourished around the seats of political power and commercial wealth in Victoria and later Vancouver, while a rural gentry took root in the pleasant landscapes of the Gulf Islands and the Okanagan, Cowichan, Comox and Kootenay valleys.

But the heartland of the establishment remained the capital and south Vancouver Island. "San Francisco on the Solent," Emily Carr called it. Terry Reksten describes it as a peculiar hybrid of English social values and American

brashness with a population that included English, Blacks, Chinese, Scots, Irish, Germans, Indians and Americans. The social scene was vigorous. For the ladies of the establishment, whether rural or urban, there were polo matches and regattas to attend, there were lawn tennis and croquet—and, of course, the round of balls, garden parties, soirees and levees where their daughters might meet the Royal Navy man with the right family connections in the Old Country. The Cowichan Valley Amateur Athletic Club, for example, boasted the best dance floor in BC. Three hundred or more could

"Everybody came to the ball. . ."

We gave a ball to the fair ladies here; two of the men-of-war the *Satellite* and *Plumper* with ourselves, determined to join together and give a grand ball to the ladies of Vancouver Island. . . the only house we could find was the market place, a most dismal-looking place, enough to drive all thoughts of dancing out of ones head, however we got all the flags we could from the ships & turned in 30 or 40 sailors & in a short time a fairy palace of flags was erected, so that not a particle of the building was visible; we then rigged up some large chandeliers & sconces of bayonets and ramrods wreathed with evergreens which when lighted up produced a regular blaze of light & made it quite a fairy scene. We also got up a large supper room in the same style & managed to provide a first-rate supper. Everybody came to the ball from the governor downwards nearly 200 in all & we kept the dancing up

Fancy dress ball at Government House in Victoria, circa 1914. Of such gatherings, Robert Melrose, a working-class man, noted wryly in his diary: "Great Ball held at Victoria, riff-raff excluded."
BC Archives G-00947

with great spirit until half past three in the morning. Everybody was quite delighted with it & it goes by the name of "the Party" par excellence; nobody says ball in this part of the world, it is always party. The ladies were very nicely dressed & some of them danced very well, they would look much better if they would only learn to wear their crinoline properly, it is most lamentable to see the objects they make of themselves, some of the hoops being quite oval, whilst others had only one hoop rather high up, the remainder of the dress hanging down perpendicularly. . .

—quoted from Lieutenant Charles Wilson's journals of service. BC Archives MS-0368

dance there and young women would row in from the Gulf Islands, waltz all night with officers from visiting warships and then row home as dawn broke.

For all the socializing, life was intensely focussed on the family. The O'Reillys perhaps best represent both their class and their time. Peter O'Reilly was Irish. He met Caroline at a dinner at the Trutches. She was described as extremely bright, vivacious and a seasoned world traveller. They were married on a snowy day in 1863 and soon had four children. But rank and privilege were no guarantee of protection from the perils that stalked everyone in an age before antibiotics and advanced medical care. Among the touching artifacts from the era held by the provincial archives is Caroline's frantic letter to Peter about the illness of their seven-year-old daughter, Mary Augusta. "My dearly beloved husband," she wrote on October 26, 1876. "I

have left writing to the last hoping that I might be able to tell you that our darling is better. I grieve to say I am not able to say so with any certainty. I am in so much anxiety that I feel difficulty to write with calmness." Mary died November 6, 1976, and is buried in Victoria.

Like most upper-class families, the O'Reillys sent the kids, Frank, Kathleen and Jack, to good schools in England to be educated. When they returned, their home at Point Ellice House was already a hive of social activity for Victoria's elite and was where Prime Minister John A. Macdonald dined during his visit to BC in 1886. The O'Reilly household was also a hotbed of Victorian romance. Daughter Kathleen had blossomed into a stunning beauty. Among her suitors was Royal Navy Captain Robert Falcon Scott, who later led the doomed British dash to the South Pole in 1912. Another suitor

Kathleen O'Reilly in flower garden at Point Ellice House, circa 1900.
BC Archives C-03922

was Lieutenant Commander Henry Scudamore Stanhope, heir to the Earldom of Chesterfield. But Kathleen spurned them both and never married. She died in 1945 at the age of 78.

Point Ellice House is a rambling structure on Victoria's Inner Harbour. It is now preserved as a museum where visitors may still take a strawberry cream tea in summer, play croquet on the lawns or walk the lovely gardens with the ghosts of Kathleen, the bold young Scott of the Antarctic, Sir John A. Macdonald, Julia Trutch, Caroline O'Reilly and the other forgotten women of the establishment.

There is, of course, no historic monument to the women consigned to the "dance halls."

10 A Rainbow Society

Most of them never met. Most of them knew little of each others' homeland. Yet women from around the world stitched their diverse cultures together across the broken landscape of this province like the panels of a many-coloured quilt. From Africa by way of the United States, from the South Sea Islands, from China and Japan, from the ghettos of Eastern Europe and from the dusty Punjab, the women who came to settle British Columbia's frontier came from everywhere. Some came in search of freedom, some came to a fate of bondage, some came as dutiful wives, some as concubines bound for a grim life in the sex trade. Some were welcomed and some were denied.

But those who came, persevered and prevailed, and embroidered upon the fabric of a new society the rich brocade of their own distinctive traditions and the experiences all women shared as wives and mothers in a patriarchal society and an unforgiving environment.

They brought their own religions and their own recipes. They modified practice in both temple and kitchen to accommodate the new realities of a different world in which they would have to nurture families and raise children. They watched those children marry across ethnic and religious boundaries, helping to bring into being the new culture that is still being forged here on the western slope of the Rockies. Descendants of those women have served as mayors and lieutenant-governors, as judges and cabinet ministers, as university chancellors and labour leaders, as intellectuals and as all-star athletes.

One of the first intersections of these varied cultures occurred on the rumpled landscape of Saltspring Island with its sheep paddocks, sunny upland meadows, pastoral lifestyle and still-liberal sensibilities. Evidence of this early multiculturalism exists in more than the genealogies of old island families. Swing

In the late 1800s the congregation of St. Paul's Church on Saltspring Island was fully integrated.
Salt Spring Archives

Above left: Hannah Estes was one of a contingent of free American Blacks who brought their families to Victoria at the invitation of James Douglas. Middle: Kini Kajiyama performing with the traditional instrument known as the koto in Cumberland, where the Japanese community built a tea garden. Right: Gracie Benjamin was one of the early Hawaiian settlers arriving in Canada in the late 1800s.
Salt Spring Archives, Estes/Stark Collection; Cumberland Museum; Salt Spring Archives, Cathy Roland Collection

left on the Ganges Road as you disembark the ferry from Vancouver Island and you'll pass one enduring symbol of that brief moment in BC's early history, when it still seemed possible to avoid the Old World prejudices and bigotry that would visit its curse on later decades: it is St. Paul's, a little stone church nestled in the shadow of Mt. Tuam at the head of Fulford Harbour. If you should take the time to look carefully at the photograph from its consecration in 1885 you will see a congregation in which, among the women at least, the white faces are far from the majority.

Among the first women from visible minorities to arrive in BC were those called Kanakas, a Polynesian word that means human beings, but which was used in a disparaging sense by white Europeans of the time. Today, however, the word has redeemed its original dignity and is used by Hawaiians themselves to refer to indigenous islanders. Disparaged or not, these Natives of what were then called the Sandwich Islands were much in demand as sailors. Tough,

Cecile Naukana, whose father William Naukana was born in the Sandwich Islands in 1813, married Ganges farmer George Napoleon Parker. This 1890s picture shows them with five of their children.
Salt Spring Archives, Cathy Roland Collection

hardy, able to navigate by the stars, consummate readers of the North Pacific weather, Kanakas were prized crewmen for the sailing captains of the late 18th and early 19th centuries. Herman Melville mentions Kanakas in his novels. When the first Kanaka women arrived on the West Coast isn't entirely clear, but we do know that one left Hawaii to accompany Frances Barkley on one leg of the 1787 voyage of discovery to Vancouver Island. Unfortunately, the young woman known as Winee became homesick and sailed for Hawaii from Macao with John Meares. She fell ill and

Maria Mahoi Douglas (later Fisher), born on the Saanich Peninsula about 1856 of a Native mother and Hawaiian father. Hawaiian families displaced from San Juan Island in 1859 settled on Saltspring Island.
Salt Spring Archives

died during the crossing of the China Sea.

During the early years of the fur trade, the number of Hawaiians working on the West Coast for the Hudson's Bay Company and arriving aboard trading vessels numbered in the many hundreds. Whether Hawaiian sailors jumped ship in BC or were marooned by captains cheating them of their wages is a matter of argument, but by the time Fort Victoria was established, they had their own street. Kanaka Row was found where the stately Empress Hotel now stands. A Kanaka Ranch was established in what's now Stanley Park and others farmed up the Fraser Valley.

But it was on Saltspring Island, where Hawaiian families displaced from San Juan Island

Mrs. Sylvia Estes Stark was born a slave and came to BC in 1857. She died in 1944 at the age of 106.
Salt Spring Archives, Estes/Stark Collection

following a boundary dispute in 1859 had resettled, that the Kanakas formed a community. One of the matriarchs was Maria Mahoi, or Mahoy, or Mahoya, depending upon the source. She'd been born about 1856 in what was then the remote, rural outback of the Saanich Peninsula. Her father was a Hawaiian, an employee of the Hudson's Bay Company, and her mother a Native woman. She was beautiful and spirited and at 15 became the "country wife" of a New England whaling captain named Abel Douglas. Maria bore seven of his children before Douglas departed. She subsequently married another Saltspring Islander, George Fisher, with whom she had six more children. Like most women of her generation, she was resourceful, self-reliant and capable of packing up the kids in a small open boat and sailing it single-handed to Sidney for a day of shopping, much like the way modern moms take the mini-van to the mall. Maria died in 1936.

Hawaiians were not the first visible minority to arrive on Saltspring Island, however. Even before the gold rush that was to transform BC, freed Black slaves from Kentucky and Mississippi had begun to settle here with the blessings of Governor James Douglas. The first arrived at Vesuvius Bay in August, 1857. By 1859 the Black community numbered more than 100. Among them was Sylvia Estes, who was born into slavery. Her father, Howard Estes, had first bought his own freedom and then his family's, paying $900 to free his daughter, before moving them to California, where the racism was cruel. Douglas sent the Black community in San Francisco an invitation to immigrate. At 20, Sylvia was already the mother of two children and pregnant with her third when she accompanied her husband, Louis Stark, to carve one of the first farms in the Gulf Islands from the bush on Saltspring near Vesuvius Bay. She died in 1944 at the age of 106.

Hard on the heels of Black and Hawaiian settlers came the first Chinese woman to BC. Mrs. Chong Lee came to Victoria with her young child in 1860 when her husband, an enterprising merchant, arrived from California to open a store. By 1868, he had a chain of shops in Barkerville, Yale, Lillooet, Quesnelle Forks and Quesnel, that advertised "groceries, provisions, rice, tea, sugar, cigars, tobacco, opium, clothing, boots and shoes, hardware and mining tools which are offered for sale at reasonable rates." His wife's arrival marked the beginning of Chinese family life on the frontier, but she was a rare sight. Although one-half of Victoria's exploding population was Chinese, in 1860 that segment was 99 percent male. By 1902, when Victoria's Chinese population was 3,283, only 96

Mrs. Lee in Victoria wearing Ching dynasty clothing circa 1910.
Glenbow Archives PA-344-2

of that number were women.

Not all of the women who came from China were respectable wives. A less scrupulous class of merchant recognized that in a society of lonely men, there was money to be made selling sex. Women from Hong Kong were brought over ostensibly to work as waitresses but soon found themselves in a world of opium addicts and prostitution. By 1883 the problem was sufficient that BC had one of its first transition houses. The Methodist Home for Chinese Girls opened in Victoria specifically to provide sanctuary for those escaping the sex trade, slavery and cruel marriage contracts.

The first Japanese woman to arrive in BC was Mrs. Washiji Oya, who followed her husband in 1887 after he came to work at Hastings Mill. She was the harbinger of a tsunami. Between her arrival and World War I, almost 20,000 immigrants would come from Japan. Men who took lonely jobs in the fishery and logging communities frequently wrote home to have parents arrange marriages with suitable women. After courtships by mail and an exchange of photographs, the "picture brides" would join them, bringing old customs to help civilize the rough male community of a new frontier. The coal mining camp of Cumberland on Vancouver Island, for

Yip Sang family members, 1906. An immigrant from China, Yip Sang worked for the CPR and later became a successful Vancouver businessman. He had 23 children—19 sons and four daughters.
Photo courtesy Henry Yip

明治武拾壱年八月渡加　　元治元年八月五日生

縣川奈神

ウヨ屋大

Mrs. Yo Oya, the first Japanese woman to settle in Canada. She came to join her husband in 1887.
Japanese Canadian National Museum

example, had both a Chinese opera house and a formal Japanese tea garden. Soon after the Japanese, Sikhs began to arrive from the Punjab, eventually founding the settlement of Paldi in the Cowichan Valley on Vancouver Island.

Not all the minorities were so easily visible, of course. A group of about 100 Jews arrived in Fort Victoria in 1858 to open businesses and, in 1863, established Canada's longest-serving synagogue. Highly educated, they soon became an essential part of the new colony's merchant and administrative establishment and their wives and daughters helped refine and civilize society in the rough frontier fort. Cecelia Davies, who had come from Australia with her prosperous parents, married Francis Sylvester in 1869 and quickly established herself as one of the capital's leading hostesses, renowned for her piano recitals. Over on the mainland, in the other would-be capital, New Westminster, Mrs. Simon Reinhardt was a social whirlwind before she moved to Victoria.

Although there was an overt anti-Semitism in some quarters, the frontier proved remarkably tolerant in some ways. In 1860, Selim Franklin was elected to BC's legislative assembly, the first Jew to hold political office in Canada. His brother Lumley was elected mayor of Victoria in 1865, the first Jew to hold such office in a North American city. He later led the Confederation movement in the new province of BC. And in 1871, Victoria elected Henry Nathan to Ottawa—the first Jew elected to the House of Commons.

Unlike Cecelia Davies and others, not all Jewish women found an easy niche in Victoria's upper crust and palatial homes in high-end neighbourhoods. Hannah Director wound up homesteading at South Fort George, where she raised three small children in a log cabin with a dirt floor. She persevered, too, becoming the first woman elected to the school board, which she eventually chaired, in Prince George. The quilt she and all these women made of their collective lives and laid upon the dramatic frontier landscape of BC still offers a profound lesson in the principles of faith, hope and charity as our province of many cultures learns to live in a climate of tolerance and mutual respect.

Hannah Director homesteaded about 35 km south of Prince George in 1914.
Jewish Historical Society of BC Archives

Old recipes and new seasonings

The frontier was nominally a man's world, but women ruled the kitchen and learned quickly to make do with what was at hand. Appetites were large, children were many and supplies were often spare, which meant relying on non-perishable staples and whatever game the shotgun and fishing rod produced to supplement the larder. As women from different backgrounds met, old recipes were spiced up with new seasonings. Here are some standard recipes that would have been a part of every pioneer-era woman's culinary repertoire. Readers who want to try a pioneer dinner can substitute chicken or turkey thighs for game birds or rabbit.

Small Bannock

3 cups flour
dash of salt
1 tsp. baking powder
2 tbsp. lard
enough water

Combine dry ingredients in bowl. Make a little well and pour in water, not too much to start. Mix into a dough and knead it. Flatten it out and put it in the greased frying pan. Cook on hot ashes over open fire or bake in a 400 degree oven. Eat it hot with bacon drippings or lard.

Smoked Salmon Soup

1 lb. smoked salmon
1 quart water
1/4 tsp. fresh ground pepper
1 cup baby spinach leaves

Break salmon into bite-sized chunks and place in large saucepan. Add water and pepper. Simmer on low heat for 15 minutes until hot. Add the spinach and cook five more minutes at simmer.

Curried Spruce Hen

2 spruce hens (you can substitute skinless, boneless chicken thighs or chunks of turkey thigh)
1/2 cup flour
4 tbsp. butter
2 medium onions, minced
1 tsp. curry powder
3 tbsp. flour
3 cups chicken broth or bouillon
1 apple, diced
salt

Skin and draw the spruce hens, cut into serving pieces, wash and drain. Melt butter in a heavy cast iron skillet. Dredge meat with flour then cook in hot fat until browned all over. Remove each piece as it browns. Cook onions in the same fat until soft and golden. Add the curry powder and stir to coat. Add the flour and stir. Add the broth and stir. Bring to a boil. Add the meat pieces and the diced apple. Cover and simmer for 90 minutes. Serve with wild rice.

Fricaseed Rabbit

1 rabbit (you can substitute 4-6 skinless, boneless chicken breasts)
1 package bacon strips
1/4 cup flour
1/4 cup butter or lard
dash salt
dash pepper
1 cup milk
1 tbsp. finely minced onion

Wrap bacon strips around each piece of meat and skewer with toothpicks. Roll in flour. Melt butter in heavy cast iron skillet or Dutch oven and brown meat. Sprinkle on salt and pepper. Add milk, pouring very slowly to keep meat from sticking to pan. Cover and simmer until tender. Remove meat and make gravy with remaining liquids. Add onion. Cook. Pour over meat.

Camp Cabbage

1 package bacon, chopped into squares
1 medium onion, chopped
1 bunch green onions, chopped
1 medium head cabbage cut into 8 pieces
3/4 cup water
1 tsp. salt
1/4 tsp. pepper

Brown the bacon in a large cast iron skillet or Dutch oven. Add onion and green onions. Cook until soft and golden. Add cabbage and sauté briefly. Add water, salt, pepper. Cover and simmer 35 minutes. Stir and serve.

Salmonberry Sweet

4 cups salmonberries
4 cups sugar

Add equal amounts of berries and sugar and slowly cook together for about 15 minutes, stirring constantly. Remove berries with slotted spoon and reserve. Boil remaining juice 15 minutes, stirring constantly. Return berries and bring back to boil, stirring constantly. Serve right away over hot biscuits.

Strong Coffee

Put 1 quart water in a clean billy-can. Add 12-16 tbsp. ground coffee. Bring to full boil then remove from heat and let stand five minutes. Add two tbsp. cold water to settle grounds. Pour and drink right away. Add sugar and canned evaporated milk to taste.

Molasses Candy

2 cups molasses
1 cup sugar
1 tbsp. vinegar
chopped walnuts
baking soda

Cook sugar and molasses together in a saucepan until it goes brittle when dropped in cold water. Stir in a pinch of baking soda and three cups of chopped walnuts. Pour onto a greased cookie sheet. Break it into pieces when cold.

11 Painters, Poets and Politicians

I n 1791, just as courageous young Frances Barkley sailed for the second time toward the uncharted coast of British Columbia, women in New Brunswick were being formally deprived of the right to vote. This exclusion of women from the political process would not end in Canada until women in Quebec finally obtained an unrestricted franchise in 1940, almost 150 years later.

But the first victory in women's long battle for political equality was won through the determination of Maria Pollard Grant, in the capital of a newly minted province that Frances Barkley could barely have imagined. Today, in a province where women have held the offices of prime minister, lieutenant-governor, premier, cabinet minister and mayor, where they sit on the bench and lead great universities, it's difficult to imagine they were once thought unfit to participate in the suffrage or political life.

Frontier women were tough enough to drive dog teams 500 kilometres at 40 below zero or to give birth alone at remote homesteads. They could skin and butcher a moose or climb the Chilkoot Pass. Yet, in the eyes of most male contemporaries they symbolized frailty and fragility—both physically and psychologically. During the pioneer era most doctors, educators and legislators defined women by their biology, creating a self-fulfilling stereotype. Before effective birth control, when women were denied full property rights and therefore had to be identified through

Women's Building at a fair in New Westminster, circa 1900. Note the banner for the Local Council of Women, an organization set up to push for political equality.
Philip Timms Collection Vancouver Public Library VPL 6692

Victoria College women's basketball team, 1912. Where women's physical recreation had previously been limited, they began to take up more robust sports.
BC Archives E-02868

their legal relationships with men—either husbands or fathers—they were made hostage to their reproductive systems. Without legal status as persons, their choices were often the economic security of marriage and its stifling social restrictions, the "freedom" of spinsterhood and economic dependence on patronizing relatives or being marginalized as women of questionable morals. And yet, for all these constraints, from the mid-19th century many women in BC were fashioning a stunning revolution in which they would transform the cultural landscape by taking up sports once reserved for men, excelling in the arts and forcing profound political reform.

Oddly enough, the year of the gold rush and the making of British Columbia was a signal year for this revolution. In 1858, an American woman created an overnight stir by climbing four kilometres to a mountain summit in Colorado. She was wearing bloomers. This daring British alternative to crinolines and starched petticoats worn by a female American mountaineer would mark the beginning of the end for the hoop skirt that women still felt compelled to wear, even on the gold diggings. Bloomers, sensible and designed by a woman, would free women to participate in active sports and eventually kill the whalebone corset, that stiff conservative symbol of control.

By 1858, women had only just begun

Unidentified woman actress photographed by Richard Maynard in the 1880s in Victoria.
BC Archives F-06219

Left: Miss Russell as Maid Marian, 1899.
BC Archives G-00170

to challenge convention and appear on the stage. A few years before, theatre in Fort Victoria was an all-male affair, usually performed by visiting Royal Navy crews. But two decades later, the Fanny Morgan Phelps Dramatic Troupe was headlining shows from Oregon to BC and performers like Lizzie Morgan, Zoe Gayton, Annie Pixley and Minnie Pixley were on their way to celebrity status. In an age before radio, television or movies, almost every town from Barkerville to

Vancouver had its own theatre, often several, including an opera house. For highbrows there were Shakespeare and readings by E. Pauline Johnson. After arriving in BC in 1894, this statuesque Mohawk poet once travelled the entire Cariboo Wagon Road to Barkerville, declaiming her romantic verse in roadhouses. She would switch from buckskins to a brocaded silk evening gown depending upon the audience. At Soda Creek she performed in a barn and her dressing room was the oat bin. The next night she performed at Lac La Hache, her silk dress still bristling with oats. But

smitten miners showered her with gold nuggets. There were sentimental melodramas, blackface minstrel shows and the erotically charged burlesques of "Klondike" Kate Rockwell, who was with the Savoy Theatrical Company in Victoria before taking her act to Dawson City in 1900.

As women reshaped the performing arts on the frontier, they were doing the

Production of _The Bridal Trap_ in Victoria, 1908. From left: Miss Stoddart as Marion, Miss H. Kent as The Marquise and Miss Carter as Rosette. BC Archives G-00198

Hannah Maynard, multiple exposure self-portrait. She pushed the limits of photography, a new technology.
BC Archives F-02850

Where women's physical recreation had previously been limited to walking, a bit of riding and occasional forays by canoe or rowboat, they began to take up more robust sports. At first these involved relatively sedate versions of lawn tennis and croquet—sports that could be played in the garments of the day. The venturesome soon took up golf and then more competitive pursuits. Women's walking competitions became popular. Women joined alpine expeditions, climbing beyond the treeline to paint and take photographs. Zoe Gayton, the actress who had warmed audiences at Victoria's New Royal Theatre, left on a cross-country hike in 1890. She crossed the United States in 213 days, averaging more than 28 kilometres per day. By the late 19th century, more than a million women in North America owned bicycles—racing them as well as riding them for errands or for touring. They raced horses, too. Isobel Stanley, whose husband was Governor General of Canada and had donated the Stanley Cup, challenged the ladies of Rideau to a hockey game against the ladies of Government House in Ottawa. Rugged team sports now had an imprimatur and there was an explosion in the number of women playing ice hockey, field hockey, baseball and lacrosse. Within a decade of the first airplane flight, Alys Bryant had qualified as a

same in the studio. As early as 1862, Victoria's Hannah Maynard was radically expanding the artistic envelope of a new technology known as photography. She had one of BC's first portrait studios and experimented with multiple exposures, perspective, mirror images, infinity and surrealism. She travelled the province—as did her husband Richard, also a photographer—for four decades, recording landscapes, portraits of people and leaving

an important photographic legacy when she died in 1918. Not far from Hannah Maynard's photo studio, a young Emily Carr was formulating the ideas that would cause her to abandon the expectations of where and how a woman should paint. Travelling to remote places on the coast alone, her bold brushwork, vibrant hues and sweeping curves would capture the fecund energy of the BC landscape as no painter before or since.

"Here was nothing but loveliness. . ."

Life Class, Westminster School of Art, 1899

The curtains of a little recess parted, out stepped the model and took her place on the throne.

I had dreaded this moment and busied myself preparing my material, then I looked up. Her live beauty swallowed every bit of my shyness. I had never been taught to think of our naked bodies as something beautiful, only as something indecent, something to be hidden.

Here was nothing but loveliness...only loveliness—a glad, life-lit body, a woman proud of her profession, proud of her shapely self, regal, illuminated, vital, high-poised above our clothed insignificance...

Every eye was upon her as she mounted the throne, fell into pose. Every student was tallying her with perfection, summing up balance, poise, spacing, movement, weight, mood.

Charcoal began to scrape upon paper and canvas... swishing lines, jagged lines, subtle curve, soft smudge.

Tremblingly my own hand lifted the charcoal—I was away, lost in the subtlety, the play of line merging into line, curve balancing curve.

—Emily Carr, in her autobiography, *Growing Pains*, Oxford University Press, 1946

**Above: Playing tennis in Vernon,
1895.**
BC Archives I-55785
**Left: Photographer Hannah Maynard
bicycles with friends in Beacon Hill
Park in Victoria in the 1890s.**
BC Archives F-05070

pilot and on July 31, 1913, became the first woman to fly over Vancouver.

Growing social acceptance of these new and expanded roles for women in everyday life was accompanied by a rising demand for political equality as well. Maria Pollard Grant used a new provincial act (passed in 1872) that extended property rights to married women to argue successfully that women who met property qualifications had the right to a vote in municipal elections. She cast her ground-breaking ballot in 1875. In 1885, she drafted a petition demanding the vote for women in BC and led a delegation to present it to the all-male legislature, a symbolic journey she would make every year until women were finally granted the franchise 32 years later. Her successful candidacy for school board was advanced by the Victoria Council of Women, organized in 1894 at a meeting presided over by Lady Ishbel Gordon, wife of Lord Aberdeen. In January of 1895, she became the first woman elected to public office in BC. Three years later, school trustee candidate Mrs. Duncan Roderick Reid became the first woman elected in Vancouver. In 1908, the Victoria Council of Women became the first in Canada to endorse the campaign for women's universal suffrage. Ten years later, BC voters would elect Mary Ellen Smith to the provincial legislature and she would become the first woman to hold cabinet rank in Canada.

If the ascent to genuine power launched the 20th century with a new beginning for women, it marked the symbolic closing of the pioneer era in BC. And yet, as the 21st century begins, it's also fair to argue that the pioneering spirit was never laid to rest and that bold women still live rugged lives in remote places, challenge conventions and continue to drive for social reforms across this vast and diverse province.

Mrs. Duncan Roderick Reid (nee Christina Campbell) was elected as Vancouver's first woman school trustee in 1898.
City of Vancouver Archives CVA Port P757 N338

12 The Last of the First

Is it true that the first non-aboriginal child born in Vancouver was a baby girl named McNeil, I was asked by Angus MacNeil of Vancouver as I plugged away at my research into the often unattributed contributions women have made to British Columbia. The archives showed that there was a Margaret Florence McNeil born in Vancouver on April 27, 1886, the year the city was both incorporated and burned down—but whether she was actually the first-born I couldn't attest. The more I asked around, the more frequently I heard in anecdotal terms that her parents had moved after the fire and she wasn't located again until 50 years later, thanks to the diligence of a city archivist who doggedly traced her to Portland, Oregon. That yarn was too good to ignore.

Then I got some unexpected help from Erin Sweeney of Richmond, who wrote to me—"at the urging of my uncle, Jake Sweeney, and my father Ed Sweeney"—to help clarify what turns out is not a mystery at all, although it began as one. And my 12-year-old daughter broke off from designing her website to track down for me a posting to a genealogical site in Cape Breton that provided some further interesting background. It was written by a Vince MacNeil, who himself thanks the research of Carol MacLean and quotes

Burned to the ground in 1886, by the late 19th century Vancouver had surpassed Victoria as the social hub of the province.
BC Archives C-05627

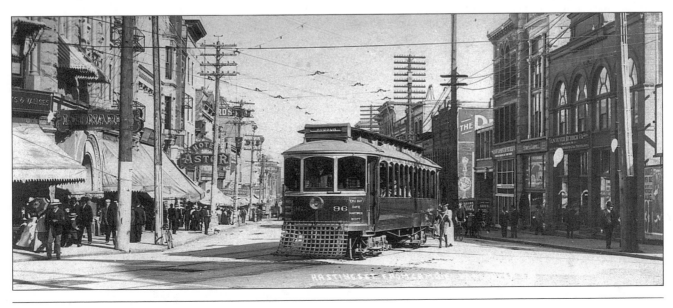

Margaret Florence McNeil, the first non-aboriginal child born in Vancouver, was tracked down by the city's archivist 54 years later and brought home for a birthday party in her honour.
City of Vancouver Archives CVA LP 129

from sources as far afield as the long-defunct *Vancouver News Herald*, the *Oban Times* in Scotland (a place I've actually visited, but only in search of the perfect Scotch) and the *Vancouver Province*.

As I say, the Vital Events Registry at the provincial archives corroborates that on April 27, 1886, exactly three weeks after the town of Granville was incorporated as the City of Vancouver and two weeks before the first meeting of the first city council—at which the first order of business was to ask Ottawa to turn over the land that would create Stanley Park—a Margaret Florence McNeil entered the world and was baptized by Father Patrick Fay at Holy Rosary, the humble predecessor of the present cathedral. The date was certainly right and the name was similar to that offered by Angus MacNeil, who wasn't sure exactly how she spelled her surname and thought she lived in Portland, Oregon, but was descended from stock on the Isle of Barra in the Outer Hebrides.

Which brought me back to Erin

Sweeney. She told me that her grandfather, M. Leo Sweeney, had served as the General Chairman of Vancouver's Diamond Jubilee. The committee apparently produced a splendid souvenir booklet of Vancouver facts from which the following excerpt is taken:

By way of contrast to the dim beginning of cities in "old" countries, there sat down to a dinner in the Stanley Park Pavilion on April 30, 1946, nine of the 16 men and women born in Vancouver in 1886.

These "Jubilarian" guests included Miss Margaret Florence McNeil, first white baby born in the year of incorporation, whose birthday was April 27, 1886. Other "1886 babies" present on this unique occasion were: A.C. Reid; C.F.H. Steele; E.G. Sumner; Mrs. Edward Brown, formerly Edna Ludlow; Mrs. W.W. Hatfield, formerly Irma Chase; Mrs. J.B. Abrams, formerly Beatrice Jagger; J.D. McPhalen; Mrs. George Sims, formerly Flora Johnston.

But there's more to this story than the birthday party that took place the year before I was born. It turns out we owe the presence of Vancouver's first-born at the celebration to the tenacity and skill of Vancouver's first city archivist, Major J.S. Matthews, a hero of Ypres who came home and had a brief stint in business before retiring in 1924. His hobby—perhaps we should say obsession—was collecting and recording early Vancouver history and, according to Donna Jean MacKinnon's short essay about him in Chuck Davis's *The Greater Vancouver Book*, his Kits Point house was soon jammed to the rafters with memorabilia. He was made the city's first archivist in 1932 and his personal collection is still at the heart of our early documentary record of the city's genesis—another triumph, I always like to point out, for the publicly spirited amateur in this age that seems overly impressed by formal credentials and the notion that you need a PhD before you can think.

Major Matthews, it seems, was blessed with an uncanny ability to remember names long-forgotten by oth-

ers and a reporter's skills in ferreting out information about them, which probably explains why he was so chummy with the reporters of his day. As I poked about looking for information, I came across letters in the papers of my late father-in-law, Bill Mayse, who was a reporter for both the *Vancouver Province* and the *Vancouver Sun* more than 75 years ago, with news tips from the archivist scrawled in the margins.

According to Vince MacNeil's posting on the Cape Breton site, the major wrote more than 900 letters in a relentless 20-year search to track down Vancouver's vanished first-born. Then a reporter drew his attention to a 1909 newspaper story that seemed to indicate that her parents, Alexander McNeil and Anna Springer McNeil, had moved to Portland after losing their home in the ferocious fire that wiped out most of Vancouver just six weeks after the baby was born. That fire was so hot it melted the church bell at St. James to cinder slag. Our intrepid archivist next wrote to the city comptroller in Portland. He obtained a municipal government list of every McNeil in the American seaport and then worked his way through the addresses. He found Margaret working as a glove buyer for a big department store.

In 1940, 54 years after her departure, the city brought her home. She was greeted at city hall by Mayor Lyle Telford, presented with a gold necklace and pendant bearing the city's coat of arms and treated to a spectacular birthday cake decorated with roses to represent Portland and a maple leaf to represent Canada. Major Matthews, who died in 1970 at the age of 92, undertook to ensure that Vancouver's long-lost birthday girl was never again forgotten. Every year until her own death in 1972, she received a cake, a present and a phone call from the City of Vancouver.

Postscript:
A Woman of Fortitude

When Linda Allison swings into the saddle of her trusted palomino, Molly, and ambles out across the rolling hills of her ranch in the Similkameen Valley to bring in calves for branding, you might be forgiven for thinking you were in the presence of an apparition. Her great-grandmother, Susan Allison, came into this valley as a girl. And now she sleeps for eternity in the family cemetery of the old Allison Ranch near Princeton, snuggled in beside her beloved husband beneath the rustling of the amber bunch grass. More than 130 years ago, Susan rode this same burnished country on Cream Kate, a horse of the same colour as Molly, for the very same purpose as the great-granddaughter who would not even be born until 12 years after the remarkable old lady was laid to rest at the age of 92.

A picture of a young Susan Allison shows her beauty, but not her adventurous spirit. From *A Pioneer Gentlewoman in British Columbias: The Recollections of Susan Allison*

"She must have been a woman of great fortitude and strong character," Linda says, relaxing after another long day tending the 200 cattle that range across almost 65 square kilometres of her deeded land and grazing leases. "I really enjoy these mountains. I always enjoy being out there. I often think if I'd been here 100 years ago [in Susan's time] how amazing it must have been to

Linda Allison, owner/operator of the Allison Creek ranch, feels a strong connection to the adventurous young woman who rode this land before her.
Glenn Baglo *Vancouver Sun*

come through this country with almost nobody here."

Susan Louisa Moir was a beautiful, vivacious teenager celebrating her fifteenth birthday when the paddlewheeler *Reliance* nosed in at a muddy landing on the Fraser River on August 18, 1860. She and her sister Jane, 17, broke away from their mother Susan and ne'er-do-well stepfather Thomas Glennie and scrambled—"joyously" was the term she later used to describe the moment—up the embankment toward the wooden palisades at Hope. The young woman, clad in the constricting corsets and puffy white petticoats that were the proper attire for proper ladies even in the wilderness, understood that she had arrived at a real frontier and that beyond it lay a vast unknown and the grand adventure that would consume the rest of her astonishing and fruitful life. This was as far as the riverboats could yet travel on the great waterway, which boiled through towering canyons. It flowed from an uncharted interior which, in many ways, was as mysterious to the newcomers as the Darkest Africa of the pulp novels that entertained city dwellers in London, Paris and Berlin.

Barely 18 months before, what became known as the Fraser Canyon War had ripped like a wildfire through the inaccessible country beyond the little settlement. When American adventurers panning for gold refused to countenance First Nations doing the same and sought to drive them off with violence, they got more than they planned. For weeks, the bodies of miners picked off from ambush had floated down the river, pitched gun battles had been fought and British arms had finally been dispatched from the Royal Navy base at Esquimalt to restore order and bring the troublemaking Americans to heel. But in 1860, more trouble was brewing at Rock Creek, where American miners refused to abide by the colonial administration's licensing rules. Governor James Douglas had ridden to the mining camp dressed in full uniform, faced down 300 surly miners in a saloon, told them flatly that he was

"He rode a superb chestnut horse. . ."

I shall never forget my first sight of a Hudson's Bay Company Brigade train coming in from Colville. I had gone for a stroll on the Hope–Similkameen trail. There were still a few berries and I was getting a "feed" when I heard bells tinkling and looking up saw a light cloud of dust from which emerged a solitary horseman, the most picturesque figure I had ever seen.

He rode a superb chestnut horse, satiny and well-groomed, untired and full of life in spite of the dust, heat and long journey. He himself wore a beautifully embroidered buckskin shirt with tags and fringes, buckskin pants, embroidered leggings and soft cowboy hat.

He was as surprised to see me as I was to see him, for he abruptly reined in his horse and stared down at me, while I equally astonished stared at him. Then, as the Bell Boy and other horses rode up, he lifted his hat and passed on. I never met him again, but was told he was a Hudson's Bay Company Officer in charge of the Colville train and that he said he was never more surprised in his life than to see a white girl on the trail—he had lived so long without seeing anyone except Indians.

—from *A Pioneer Gentlewoman in British Columbia: The Recollections of Susan Allison*, edited by Margaret Ormsby, University of BC Press, 1976

building them a road from Hope but that they had damn well better abide by the law or he'd be back with 500 Royal Marines to give them a taste of British justice.

Doubtless, the air was still electric with tension when Susan took her first walk through the Native village adjacent to the little settlement, marvelling over the bales of salmon dried for winter, the beautifully patterned dog-hair blankets and the intricate baskets, so tightly woven she could carry water in them. Inadvertently, this friendly, curious, irrepressible girl found herself mingling with the who's who of high society in the new colony of British Columbia, itself not yet two years old. At Fort Victoria, she'd already been introduced to Douglas, to the governor's charming son-in-law Dr. John Helmcken and his wife Cecilia and to the tolerant, reform-minded Reverend Edward Cridge of Christ Church Cathedral. Travelling with her on the riverboat were Judge Matthew Bailey Begbie, Lieutenant Colonel Richard Moody and Edgar Dewdney, the future lieutenant-governor who was then a young surveyor about to embark upon the building of the promised wagon road from Hope through the Similkameen that would make his name. Dewdney would soon be so smitten with Susan's older sister that his mooning

over her became a source of ribald amusement among the fur traders, merchants and Royal Engineers in the little community. But he was determined, love prevailed and he successfully courted and, in 1864, married Jane. Waiting on the riverbank as the two excited girls scrambled up in 1860 were Peter O'Reilly, the witty Irish surveyor whose home would become the centre of social life in the capital, and William Yates, the canny entrepreneur whose name now graces one of Victoria's main streets.

The unpretentious teenager, rather than being intimidated by her physical and social surroundings, absorbed her encounters with them with such intensity that decades later her memoirs still crackle with the vividness of her impressions, with the sense of awe, wonder and privilege at what she was witnessing and of which she had become part. Her dreams of adventure were soon tempered by the reality of the endeavour upon which she had embarked and for which neither she nor her gentrified parents were very well equipped. Her stepfather had squandered the family fortune yet still had delusions of setting himself up as a country squire in the colonies. "None of us knew how to wash clothes," she wrote. "We had a tin tub that we brought out with us that we used for a wash tub and as we were ignorant as to

Susan Allison's older sister Jane met and married a young British engineer who was building a wagon road at Hope. Edgar Dewdney was later appointed Lieutenant-Governor of BC and Jane became Chatelaine.
BC Archives A-01179

the use of wash boards, we bent over the bath and rubbed with our hands until they bled and our backs felt broken. As we always wore white embroidered petticoats, we had rather a bad time on washing day." Baking bread, one essen-

tial skill of frontier life, proved a daunting mystery until a trailwise man named Kilburn taught Susan how to make sourdough and bake it in a skillet. She learned how to sew and found there was a market for petticoats in the muddy settlement. She taught school.

And she met a young miner named John Allison who had learned Chinook, was on friendly terms with the Natives and had been venturing inland on the fur brigade trail where he had taken a 65-hectare homestead near Vermilion Forks at the confluence of the Tulameen and Similkameen rivers. The "red earth" from which the place took its name was in great demand for ceremonial paint by the Okanagan, the Shuswap and even the fierce and much-feared Blackfeet, who were then engaged in a bitter war with the Americans across what is now Montana. The Natives visited the ochre deposits often, but they considered Allison a friend. He'd quickly discovered

The Allison children pose with dogs and horses in the Similkameen Valley. Susan Allison gave birth to 14 children, the last at age 47. All of the children lived to maturity.
BC Archives D-08228

Susan Allison rests in an armchair in the outdoors she loved so much.
BC Archives A-06557

there was more satisfaction in raising cattle and driving them to the coast than there was in chasing gold dust. He spent most of his time in the saddle, so perhaps it was not unexpected that the handsome young man had soon given the pretty teenager the horse she named Cream Kate and was teaching her to ride.

One evening, riding with him at dusk, she realized she must get home to mother before dark or there'd be hell to pay, so she set out at a brisk canter while he continued to his destination at Powder Camp. She was knocked from her horse by a branch, her skirt snagged on the saddle horn and she was dragged for two kilometres with the horse kicking her all the way. Finally, the skirt tore off and she stumbled to a neighbour's house. Fortunately, her mother was away and the neighbour was discreet and didn't report her bruises and state of dress the next day.

In any event, the experience didn't dampen the romance and when John proposed to her during one of his cattle drives in 1868, she accepted and set out with her new husband to his remote ranch beyond the mountains. "Then began my camping days and the wild, free life I ever loved till age and infirmity put an end to it," she would write fondly when she was near 80. "On the journey out we rode the two Kates, Cream and Grey. My husband sent the three packboys on ahead to fix camp...

"I went to the creek and washed and did up my hair in the darkness and when I regained the camp, Tuc-tac had spread a canvas in front of the fire with fried trout, grouse, bacon and bannock. That was washed down with tin cups of delicious-tasting tea. We sat and talked until late, the Indian boys sitting with us and telling us stories of the place."

Her husband and the ranch hands were often away on cattle drives or tending the livestock. With only the local Native women for companionship she soon decided she must learn Chinook, did so, and became an important authority on the aboriginal customs, folklore, legends and history in the Similkameen Valley. She found that the role of a rancher's wife on the frontier was variable. At times she served as hostess to travellers—General William Tecumseh Sherman, the US Civil War hero, passed by and presented her seven-year-old son with his sword after a demonstration of horsemanship—as well as postmistress, fur trader and bookkeeper. In addition were the usual cooking, housekeeping and child rearing duties, of which there were many. Without the benefit of medical assistance and with only her husband and a Native midwife in attendance, Susan Allison gave birth to 14 children, the last at the age of 47, all of whom lived to maturity.

When the Allisons held a big family reunion several years ago, more than 300 of her descendants turned up. Today, the bloodlines established by this remarkable frontier woman reach across both BC's landscape and our pioneer history. Perhaps the most poignant is the one that now resides in the clear, steady gaze of Linda, the great-granddaughter she never knew, a woman astride a pale horse just like her own, riding across the beautiful, still-empty landscape where Susan Allison's spirited dreams have fused with the eternal earth of British Columbia.

Afterword

In the sun-burnished August of 1914, as trains laden with excited recruits bound for the First World War wound their way through the Interior, young women in big hats and white summer dresses would make their way down to the station stops with baskets of cherries for the laughing, khaki-clad soldiers. Did those women imagine, then, that half those handsome young men would become casualties; that none would return unmarked in mind or spirit? The image lingers as a poignant metaphor. For, as the remarkable era covered in this book drew to a close and British Columbia slid toward the bloody engagements that would irrevocably transform the province, most women still stood at the margins of public life as they had once stood on the fringes of a wild frontier.

True, a few had been elected to school boards and a few had voted in municipal elections—if they met the stringent rules that defined them as land owners. Some had carved out a niche as activists and intellectuals. Increasingly women moved into the work force and would soon do so in unprecedented numbers as the war claimed more and more of the male population. Yet for all their profound contributions to the shaping of BC, women were still denied the vote in general elections at both federal and provincial levels. Few outside the upper classes had the benefit of a higher education. For those who did, education was largely viewed as an accessory to life in cultured society. Even to women of means, the university-trained professions remained essentially closed. Women were not expected to pursue careers—or even to wish to—but rather to dedicate themselves to making homes for families.

And yet in the years that lay ahead, those women, their daughters and their granddaughters would turn their efforts to reshaping the social, political and economic landscapes yet again. By 1917, the suffrage movement had finally obtained the vote—although only for some. Women of Chinese, Japanese, Hindu, First Nations and Doukhobor descent were still denied the franchise and would continue to be denied it for another 30 years or more.

Still, in a by-election held on January 24, 1918, Mary Ellen Smith of Vancouver became the first woman to run for a seat in the provincial legislature. She won. In the general election of 1920, one of three female candidates among 155 province-wide, she went on to top the Vancouver polls and was rewarded with a cabinet post, the first ever held by a woman in the British Empire.

Today, BC women have achieved acclaim in politics, science, the arts, sports, industry and commerce. A BC woman has served as prime minister of Canada. Another as premier of the province. Yet another as lieutenant-governor. Women serve in senior cabinet posts and as First Nations chiefs, as supreme court justices and as mayors of cities big and small. They lead powerful labour unions and run major corporations. They work as plumbers and software designers, systems analysts and university presidents. They are award-winning novelists and newspaper editors, poets and historians, medical researchers and deep ocean scientists, pilots and police detectives, visual artists and mathematicians, mountaineers and movie stars, musicians and Olympic champions.

Where higher education was once the nearly exclusive preserve of men, women have made it their highway to success. In 2003, girls outnumbered boys among graduates of BC's public education system and 83 per cent who entered kindergarten graduated from grade 12. Over half the graduates of universities are now women. One in three graduates in higher mathematics is now a woman.

Few young women contemplating a career today regard any field as being closed to them. This confident sense of entitlement—which may be the most significant gift that any generation can bestow upon its successors—they owe to those grandmothers and great-grandmothers who encountered an often unforgiving frontier, confronted its turbulence and change and from it shaped the world of marvels their great-granddaughters now inherit.

Source Notes

Page 74. Reprinted with permission of the publisher from *A Pioneer Gentlewoman in British Columbia: The Recollections of Susan Allison* by Margaret A. Ormsby © University of British Columbia Press 1976. All rights reserved by the publisher.

Page 37. Exhibit notes are reprinted with permission of the Clallam County Historical Society, Port Angeles, Washington.

Pages 41,42,44. Selections from Tape 4032 are reprinted with permission of the BC Archives.

Page 56. Selections from Archives MS-0368 are reprinted with permission of the BC Archives.

Pages 30, 53. Reprinted with permission of the author from *Barkerville: A Gold Rush Experience* by Richard Thomas Wright (Winter Quarters Press, 1998).

Pages 21, 22. Reprinted with permission of the publisher from *The Remarkable World of Frances Barkley 1769–1845* by Beth Hill with Cathy Converse (Touch Wood Editions 2003).

Page 47. Reprinted with permission of the author from *Their Own History: Women's Contribution to the Labour Movement of British Columbia* by Betty Griffin and Susan Lockhart (United Fishermen and Allied Workers' Union and CAW Seniors Club, 2002).

Page 49. Reprinted with permission of the publisher from *Women of British Columbia* by Jan Gould (Hancock House, 1975).

Page 68. Reprinted from *Growing Pains* by Emily Carr (Oxford University Press, 1946).

Page 17. Excerpt from "At Birth" by Mary Augusta Tappage from *The Days of Augusta* © 1973, 1992 by Augusta Evans and Jean E. Speare. Published by Douglas & McIntyre Ltd. Reprinted with permission of the publisher.

Bibliography

Akrigg, G.P.V. and Helen B. *British Columbia Chronicle, 1778–1846; 1847–1871*, 2 vols. Vancouver: Discovery Press, 1977.

Axtell, James. *Natives and Newcomers: The Cultural Origins of North America*. London: Oxford University Press, 2001.

Barman, Jean. *The West Beyond the West: A History of British Columbia*. Toronto: University of Toronto Press, 1996.

Bowen, Lynne. *Boss Whistle: The Coal Miners of Vancouver Island Remember*. Nanaimo: Nanaimo and District Museum and Rocky Point Books, rev. ed., 2002.

Bowes, Gordon E., ed. *Peace River Chronicles: Eighty-One Eye-Witness Accounts from the First Exploration in 1793 of the Peace River Region of British Columbia, Including the Finlay and the Parsnip River Basins*. Vancouver: Prescott Publishing Company, 1963.

Carr, Emily. *Growing Pains: The Autobiography of Emily Carr*. Toronto: Oxford University Press, 1946.

Davis, Chuck. *The Greater Vancouver Book: An Urban Encyclopaedia*. Vancouver: Linkman Press, 1997.

de Bertrand Lugrin, N. *The Pioneer Women of Vancouver Island, 1843–1866*. John Hosie, ed. Victoria: Women's Canadian Club of Victoria, 1928.

Fish, Gordon, ed. "Dreams of Freedom: Bella Coola, Cape Scott, Sointula." *Sound Heritage Series*, Vol 36. Victoria: Public Archives of BC, 1982.

Francis, Daniel, ed. *Encyclopedia of British Columbia* Madeira Park: Harbour Publishing, 2000.

Glavin, Terry and Former Students of St. Mary's. *Amongst God's Own: The Enduring Legacy of St. Mary's Mission*. Mission, BC: Longhouse Publishing, 2002.

Gould, Jan. *Women of British Columbia*. Saanichton: Hancock House Publishers, 1975.

Griffin, Betty and Susan Lockhart. *Their Own History: Women's Contribution to the Labour Movement of British Columbia*. Vancouver: United Fishermen and Allied Workers' Union and CAW Seniors Club, 2002.

Gunther, Erna. *Indian Life on the Northwest Coast of North America as Seen by the Early Explorers and Fur Traders during the Last Decades of the Eighteenth Century*. Chicago: Univ of Chicago Press, 1972.

Hamilton, Bea. *Salt Spring Island*. Vancouver: Mitchell Press Ltd., 1969.

Hill, Beth and Cathy Converse. *The Remarkable World of Frances Barkley, 1769 – 1845*. Victoria: Touch Wood Editions, 2003.

Ito, Roy. *The Japanese Canadians*. Van Nostrand Reinhold Ltd., 1978.

Johnson, Peter. *Voyages of Hope: The Saga of the Bride-Ships*. Victoria: Touch Wood Editions, 2002.

Knight, Rolf. *Indians at Work: An Informal History of Native Labour in British Columbia 1858–1930*. Vancouver: New Star Books, 1996.

Koppel, Tom. *Kanaka: The Untold Story of Hawaiian Pioneers in British Columbia and the Pacific Northwest*. North Vancouver: Whitecap Books, 1995.

Leonoff, Cyril Edel. *Pioneers, Pedlars and Prayer Shawls: The Jewish Communities in British Columbia and the Yukon.* Victoria: Sono Nis Press, 1978.

Light, Beth and Alison Prentice. *Pioneer and Gentlewomen of British North America, 1713–1867.* New Hogtown Press: 1980.

Meilleur, Helen. *A Pour of Rain: Stories from a West Coast Fort.* Victoria: Sono Nis, 1980.

Mitchell, David and Dennis Duffy, eds. "Bright Sunshine and a Brand New Country: Recollections of the Okanagan Valley, 1890–1914." *Sound Heritage Series,* Vol 8, No 3. Victoria: Public Archives of BC, 1979.

Perry, Adele. *On the Edge of Empire: Gender, Race and the Making of British Columbia, 1849–1871.* Toronto: Univ of Toronto Press, 2001.

Reksten, Terry. *More English than the English: A Very Social History of Victoria.* Victoria: Orca Book Publishers, 1986.

Smith, Jessie Ann. *Widow Smith of Spence's Bridge.* As told to J. Meryl Campbell and Audrey Ward. Murphy Shewchuk, ed. Merritt, BC: Sonotek Publishing, 1989.

Tappage, Mary Augusta. *Days of Augusta.* Jean E. Speare, ed. Vancouver: J.J. Douglas, 1973.

Toynbee, Richard Mouat. *Snapshots of Early Salt Spring and Other Favoured Islands.* Ganges, BC: Mouat's Trading Company Ltd., 1978.

Walbran, J.T. *British Columbia Coast Names, 1592–1906.* Vancouver: J.J. Douglas, 1971.

White, Howard, ed. *Raincoast Chronicles First Five.* Madeira Park: Harbour Publishing, 1977.

White, Howard, ed. *Raincoast Chronicles Six/Ten.* Madeira Park: Harbour Publishing, 1983.

Wright, Allan A. *Prelude to Bonanza: The Discovery and Exploration of the Yukon.* Sidney, BC: Gray's Publishing, 1976.

Wright, Richard Thomas. *Barkerville, Williams Creek, Cariboo: A Gold Rush Experience.* Winter Quarters Press, 1998.

Index